ORIOLE PARK BRANCH
DATE DUE 2/06

MAR 1 5 2000			
MAY 2 4 2000			
JUN 0 7 2000			
NOV 3 0 2001			
MAY 0 8 2002			
MAR 3 1 2003			
AUG 1 6 2005			

DEMCO 38-296

P9.35

THE SALEM WITCHCRAFT TRIALS IN AMERICAN HISTORY

Other titles *in American History*

The Alamo
in American History
(ISBN 0-89490-770-0)

Alcatraz Prison
in American History
(ISBN 0-89490-990-8)

The Battle of the Little Bighorn
in American History
(ISBN 0-89490-768-9)

The Boston Tea Party
in American History
(ISBN 0-7660-1139-9)

The California Gold Rush
in American History
(ISBN 0-89490-878-2)

The Fight for Women's
Right to Vote
in American History
(ISBN 0-89490-986-X)

The Great Depression
in American History
(ISBN 0-89490-881-2)

The Industrial Revolution
in American History
(ISBN 0-89490-985-1)

Japanese-American Internment
in American History
(ISBN 0-89490-767-0)

John Brown's Raid
on Harpers Ferry
in American History
(ISBN 0-7660-1123-2)

The Mormon Trail and
the Latter-day Saints
in American History
(ISBN 0-89490-988-6)

The Lincoln Assassination
in American History
(ISBN 0-89490-886-3)

McCarthy and the Fear of
Communism in American History
(ISBN 0-89490-987-8)

Native Americans and the
Reservation in American History
(ISBN 0-89490-769-7)

The Oregon Trail
in American History
(ISBN 0-89490-771-9)

The Panama Canal
in American History
(ISBN 0-7660-1216-6)

The Salem Witchcraft Trials
in American History
(ISBN 0-7660-1125-9)

The Transcontinental Railroad
in American History
(ISBN 0-89490-882-0)

The Underground Railroad
in American History
(ISBN 0-89490-885-5)

The Watergate Scandal
in American History
(ISBN 0-89490-883-9)

THE SALEM WITCHCRAFT TRIALS IN AMERICAN HISTORY

David K. Fremon

Enslow Publishers, Inc.

40 Industrial Road   PO Box 38
Box 398   Aldershot
Berkeley Heights, NJ 07922   Hants GU12 6BP
USA   UK
http://www.enslow.com

Library of Congress Cataloging-in-Publication Data

Fremon, David K.
     The Salem witchcraft trials in American history / David K. Fremon.
        p. cm. — (In American history)
     Includes bibliographical references and index.
     Summary: Discusses the issues and controversy surrounding
the trials, highlighting possible causes and the key figures.
     ISBN 0-7660-1125-9
     1. Trials (Witchcraft)—Massachusetts—Salem—Juvenile literature.
2. Salem (Mass.)—History—Colonial period, ca. 1600–1775—Juvenile
literature. [1. Trials (Witchcraft)—Massachusetts—Salem. 2. Salem
(Mass.)—History—Colonial period, ca. 1600–1775.] I. Title. II. Series.
KFM2478.8.W5F74   1999
345.744'50288—DC21
                                                                    98-6240
                                                                      CIP
                                                                       AC

Printed in the United States of America

10 9 8 7 6 5 4 3 2

To Our Readers:
All Internet addresses in this book were active and appropriate when we
went to press. Any comments or suggestions can be sent by e-mail to
Comments@enslow.com or to the address on the back cover.

Illustration Credits: Courtesy Peabody Essex Museum, Salem, Mass.,
pp. 9, 20, 25, 27, 34, 104; David K. Fremon, pp. 116, 117, 118; Dover
Pictorial Archives, pp. 12, 17, 99; Enslow Publishers, Inc., pp. 40, 63;
Library of Congress, pp. 57, 74, 80, 89, 97, 106.

Cover Illustration: T. H. Matteson, "The Accusation of George Jacobs,
August 5, 1692," Oil on Canvas, 1855, Library of Congress; Dover
Pictorial Archives; Courtesy of Peabody Essex Museum, Salem, Mass.

★ CONTENTS ★

"WHAT SIN HATH GOD FOUND IN ME?"

Rebecca Nurse stared quietly at the judges in the courtroom. Her friends, family members, and many curious onlookers, were packed inside Salem's meeting-house. Several doctors, merchants, and town leaders also crowded into the building. But the front row was reserved for the guests of honor— adolescent girls who had accused Rebecca Nurse of being a witch.

It would be hard to find a more unlikely suspect. For more than seventy years, the gentle woman had served as a model of Puritan behavior. She did not even complain when told of the witchcraft accusations. Instead, she asked, "What sin hath God found in me unrepented of that he should lay such an affliction on me in my old age?"[1]

Yet now dire charges faced her. The girls who accused her said she floated into their bedrooms at night. Another witness, Ann Putnam, Sr., who some believe was mentally unstable, testified that Rebecca Nurse had tried to force them to sign the devil's book and give up their souls. When Putnam refused, she said that Nurse "threatened to tear my soul out of my body."[2] No one claimed that the frail woman physically did these things. Instead, they charged that her specter (spirit) was responsible.

The jury weighed the evidence. On the one hand, there was Nurse's lifetime of good works and testimony from her friends. On the other hand, there were incredible accusations coming mainly from the mouths of children.

As a silent courtroom listened, jury foreman Thomas Fiske announced the panel's decision. Rebecca Nurse was . . . not guilty!

"Immediately all the accusers in the court, and suddenly after all the afflicted out of court, made a hideous outcry, to the amazement not only of the spectators but the court also," wrote observer Robert Calef.[3] They began screeching, rolling on the floor, kicking, and thrashing their bodies. A moment ago, the room had a churchly silence. Now it became a madhouse.

Chief Judge William Stoughton asked the jury to reconsider. He reminded them of something Rebecca Nurse had said. When accused witch Deliverance Hobbs was brought in to court to testify, Nurse had said, "Why do they bring her? She is one of us."[4]

Fiske said he did not remember the statement. He asked Rebecca Nurse to repeat it. Nurse, partially deaf and tired from the long trial, did not hear him. She did not respond.

A nineteenth-century painting by artist T. H. Matteson, "Examination of a Witch," shows the chaos that reigned during the Salem witchcraft trials.

The jury deliberated again. This time they came up with a guilty verdict. Rebecca Nurse, until now known for her kindness, was sentenced to die.

Rebecca Nurse's trial might seem bizarre, but it was not unique in 1692. Before the year ended, nineteen persons would be hanged, one would be tortured to death, and others would die in prison. Judges and accusers hoped to rid New England of evil. Instead, their actions became a symbol of injustice—the Salem witchcraft trials.

2

"THOU SHALT NOT SUFFER A WITCH TO LIVE"

Ever since prehistoric times, people have pondered the unknown. Men and women could see, hear, smell, taste, and touch the world around them. But sometimes those five senses could not answer all of the world's questions. Some things—comets, earthquakes, eclipses, diseases—were beyond the understanding of the ancients. When natural explanations were not available, people turned to supernatural ones.

Gods and demons had powers beyond those of humans. But even some humans appeared to perform supernatural acts. These people were known as wizards, sorcerers, sorceresses, and witches.

"A Society That Believes in Witchcraft"

Television and movies give us an image of a witch—an ugly old woman dressed in black, wearing a pointed hat, riding on a broomstick, cackling, and casting evil spells. But there were many kinds of witches who performed several different roles.

Societies often welcomed those with extraordinary powers. One who practiced white (good) magic was respected. Witches or sorcerers could assure a good harvest, promise victory in war, bring rain, or cure an ailing child.

But powers could be used for evil as well as good. Many believed a witch could kill a neighbor's livestock or crops. If a family member suddenly died, neighbors might blame a witch's black magic.

Did these witches actually have powers to change the forces of the world? Not really. But they were able to convince others that they had such powers. "In a society which believes in witchcraft, it works," author Chadwick Hansen noted.[1]

Men, women, or children could be witches. But throughout history, many more women than men have been accused of witchcraft. Church leaders often accused witches of being the devil's lovers. Male church leaders also claimed women were more likely to become witches, because they believed women were weaker and less intelligent than men.[2]

Ancient Witches

Ancient mythology abounds with stories of beings who appeared to have supernatural powers. Sumerians and Babylonians in the Middle East believed the world was full of hostile spirits. Many of these spirits, such as the powerful Lilitu, were believed to be female.

Witches were believed to have supernatural powers, such as the power to bring on a storm.

Greek goddesses often possessed dark, mysterious traits. Medusa, queen of the Gorgons, had hair made of snakes and a stare that could turn men to stone.

Romans also expressed fear of witches and sorcerers. Hecate, queen of the underworld, could drive men mad. Sacrifices of honey cakes and chicken hearts were offered to keep her away.

Witches and the Devil

According to legend, Roman Emperor Constantine saw a vision of a cross before the Battle of Milvian

Bridge in 312 A.D. He won the battle and adopted Christianity as his religion. Later emperors followed his example. By the end of the fourth century, Christianity had become the official Roman religion.

The devil played an essential part in early Christianity. The Christian Church was fighting an all-out war to rid the world of Satan and his followers. Witches were considered part of Satan's forces. The Church accused them of engaging in many kinds of sinful behavior. Supposedly, witches gathered in meetings called *sabbats*, where they took part in wild orgies, practiced cannibalism, and made fun of Christian sacraments. Witches could change themselves into frogs or fireflies, or make themselves invisible. They kept familiars, imps in the shape of animals or birds. From marks on their bodies known as witches' teats, witches suckled those familiars. They flew across the countryside on animals or poles. In these forms, they could wreak havoc on enemies or neighbors.

Witches were believed to be against God. The Bible, in the book of Exodus, declared "Thou shalt not suffer [permit] a witch to live."[3] Therefore, witches had to be eliminated.

In 1231, the Roman Catholic Church took official action against witches. It started the Inquisition, a court that enforced the Church's laws. Inquisitions sought to convict heretics (people who opposed the Church's views). They seized a suspect's property, then imprisoned and executed him or her. These Church courts required minimal evidence. Rules made it easy to prove a defendant guilty, and nearly impossible for anyone to defend himself or herself.

Inquisitors used any method to get confessions, even torture. Most victims confessed, and many named other suspects. The court then went after those people.

Spain's was the most infamous inquisition. The Spanish Inquisition persecuted Moors (Muslims), Jews, witches, and others. But Spain was not alone in its attacks. From the thirteenth to eighteenth centuries, inquisitions caused hundreds of thousands of deaths.

"I Would Burn All of Them"

In 1517, a German priest named Martin Luther nailed a paper to the Wittenburg Church door. This was no ordinary document. Luther opposed several beliefs and practices of the Roman Catholic Church. His Ninety-five Theses became a starting point of the Protestant Reformation.

Throughout northern and western Europe, Protestant groups came into conflict with Catholics. These disagreements often led to war. For more than two centuries, Europe became a religious battleground.

Luther disagreed with many Catholic doctrines. However, he accepted the Catholic position on witches. He said, "I would burn all of them."[4] John Calvin, another Protestant leader, also called for witches to be burned to death. Protestants attacked presumed witches with just as much ferocity as did Catholics.

While Catholic inquisitions were strongest in southern European countries, Protestants acted with equal harshness in northern Europe. Many Christians there still engaged in various pagan practices. They danced around bonfires, had orgies, and consulted fortune-tellers. Others worshipped gods of the forests and fields. To many religious leaders, these pagan practices were heretical. Such actions called for death.

Witchcraft in Europe

Not everyone charged with witchcraft was innocent. Throughout Europe, many people practiced forbidden arts, using spells or incantations to change the world. And not all of these would-be witches tried to help their fellow beings. Many cast spells to cause sickness, injury, or death to neighbors or rulers. Some used local superstitions about witchcraft for profit. So-called storm makers roamed from village to village. Peasants paid these con artists to keep deluges from their fields.

Most accused people, however, were innocent of witchcraft. Some were victims of vindictive neighbors. Other accused witches opposed the prevailing local religion. Still others were victims of mass hysteria.

Innocent or not, the accused suffered. An estimated two hundred thousand suspected witches were accused and about one hundred thousand were executed. Often, the accusations took place on a large scale. In some Swiss villages, nearly all women were executed. One prosecutor, Benedict of Carpyou, Saxony, ordered twenty thousand deaths. Five thousand burned in the French province of Alsace. The anti-witch fervor spread into Scotland. More than thirty-four hundred suspected witches died there between 1580 and 1680.

Those responsible for these deaths felt they were doing the world a favor. God-fearing people were not safe with witches on the loose. Removing an agent of Satan might save many souls. They even felt they were doing the witches a favor. Whether the witch was performing wicked acts or not, he or she was completely under Satan's power. The witch's soul was doomed to eternal damnation in hell. There was only one way such a person could be saved. He or she would have to repent of his or her sins before being executed.

Witchcraft in England

King Henry VIII of England wanted a son. His father had risen to the English throne following a bloody civil war. He wanted to avoid a similar turmoil. Many people in the mid-sixteenth century would not see a daughter as a rightful heir. For the sake of his country, he needed a male heir. His longtime wife, Catherine of Aragon, had failed to provide that son. She was now past child-bearing age. If Henry were to have a son, it would have to be with another woman.

Henry sought an annulment, a ruling from the Roman Catholic Church that would say the marriage never existed. Pope Clement VII refused the request. Since the Catholic Church would not permit a divorce, Henry VIII took matters into his own hands. He

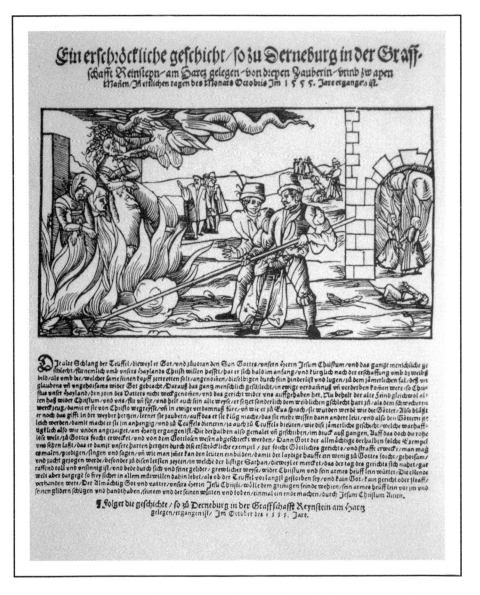

A fear of witchcraft existed throughout both Europe and America, with many people executed, often burned at the stake, for being suspected witches. In America, most witches were hanged, rather than burned.

declared an independent Church of England, with himself as its leader. Henry then divorced Catherine, and remarried. This action led to religious turmoil in England that would last more than a century.

Henry's subsequent marriages produced only one son. Edward VI, a frail child, survived his father, but died at age sixteen in 1553. Bloody religious disputes followed the young king's death. Edward's successor, his sister Mary, tried to bring England back to Catholicism. When she died, her sister, Elizabeth, followed their father's Church of England.

Elizabeth's death in 1603 brought another king. James VI of Scotland became James I of a united England and Scotland. But this political unity did not bring about spiritual harmony. Religious strife in England would have a great impact on the American colonies later in the century.

James strongly believed in witchcraft. Before he became king of England, he had written a book called *Daemonologie*. In it he claimed, "Assaults of Satan are most certainly practiced and that the instruments thereof merit most severely to be punished."[5] His King James version of the Bible used the word *witch* more than earlier versions did. He ordered a new law against witchcraft in 1604. Under James, more witches were hanged than under any other English monarch.

But even under James, England was more tolerant of witches than the rest of Europe. Four out of five accused witches were acquitted or sent to prison. Those

SOURCE DOCUMENT

HOW LONG HAVE YOU BEEN A WITCH?

WHY DID YOU BECOME A WITCH?

HOW DID YOU BECOME A WITCH, AND WHAT DID YOU DO ON THE OCCASION?

WHAT DEMONS AND OTHER HUMANS PARTICIPATED [AT THE SABBAT]?

HOW WAS THE SABBAT BANQUET ARRANGED?

WHAT INJURY DID YOU DO TO SUCH-AND-SUCH PERSON, AND HOW DID YOU DO IT?

WHO ARE THE CHILDREN ON WHOM YOU HAVE CAST A SPELL?

WHAT IS THE OINTMENT WITH WHICH YOU RUB YOUR BROOMSTICK MADE OF?[6]

In the Middle Ages, people accused of witchcraft were assumed guilty unless they could prove themselves innocent. These are the kinds of questions asked during a witchcraft trial.

sentenced to death met a quicker and less torturous end. English witches were hanged, not burned to death.

"What . . . Knavery Is Practiced Against These Old Women"

During the European witch-hunt hysteria, most people believed in witchcraft. Even if those condemned to death knew their own innocence, many still thought there were witches who hexed other people.

Not everyone, however, agreed with witch-hunts and witch trials. Friedrich von Spee, a Jesuit official, spoke out against torture and called for reasonable

Matthew Hopkins, the self-proclaimed "Witchfinder General" of England, brought hundreds of suspected witches to trial in the 1640s.

trials. In 1584 Englishman Reginald Scot wrote in *Discoverie of Witchcraft*, "What abominable and devilish inventions, and what flat and plain knavery is practiced against these old women."[7]

Despite such arguments, witch-hunt fever continued into the seventeenth century. For some, it was a profitable business. From 1644 until 1646, a soldier of fortune named Matthew Hopkins brought at least two hundred accused witches to trial. He sometimes used starvation, sleep deprivation, or other tortures to get confessions.

Judges were more than willing to believe Hopkins, the self-proclaimed "Witchfinder General of England." But even Hopkins had his limits. His methods aroused popular opposition, and he died in disgrace in 1647.

By the mid-seventeenth century, witch-hunts were on the decline. In some cases, science was able to answer supernatural questions. Churches relied less on belief in supernatural events and more on natural laws. Courts relied more on physical evidence and less on spectral (supernatural) evidence. Leading clergy also lost their enthusiasm for witchcraft persecutions.

Witchcraft hysteria, however, did not completely die. Its seed was carried to America by a group of religious refugees who called themselves Puritans.

3

"CITY ON A HILL"

John Winthrop strolled along the deck of the *Arabella* as it crossed the Atlantic Ocean. As leader of the group sailing to New England in 1630, he knew what had to be done. "We must be knit together in this work as one man. . . . " he told his fellow passengers. "We must delight in . . . our community as members of the same body."[1]

Winthrop was bringing no ordinary group of colonists to America. They were Puritans, religious refugees from England. "We are entered into Covenant with [God] for this work," he claimed.[2] In America, they would fight a battle with God against the devil.

If righteousness would prevail, Winthrop believed, individual members had to make sacrifices. Each community must be a body, and individuals must not regard themselves as more important than the community. "The good of the whole overpasses any person's individual need," Winthrop commented.[3]

"Stay Not Among the Wicked"

The Puritans felt they had no choice but to leave Europe. The religious state of England was too corrupt for their views.

Queen Elizabeth I had tried to ease tensions between Protestants and Catholics in England. Under Elizabeth, the Church of England allowed priests to marry. But it kept Catholic features such as holy days, choral music, and a rigid church hierarchy. Elizabeth's attempts at compromise did not satisfy many Protestants. One group, called the Puritans, wanted to purify the English church by ridding it of Catholic rituals.

When Elizabeth died, King James kept the Church of England. The English church still had Catholic rituals with the king, rather than the pope, as the head of the church. James had little use for the Puritans. Once in power, he ordered Puritan ministers removed from their pulpits. He once wrote a friend that he had "peppered the Puritans soundly."[4] In this environment, the Puritans could not feel welcome.

A ballad urged the Puritans to worship God on the distant shores of America:

> *Stay not among the wicked*
> *Lest that with them you perish*
> *But let us to New England go*
> *And the pagan people cherish.*[5]

In March 1630, fifteen ships holding a thousand colonists responded to that invitation. These were not young, idle adventurers. Most were middle-aged and older. They were skilled, respectable, and devout citizens. They brought as many belongings as possible with them: cattle, sheep, pigs, goats, seeds, shovels, hoes, pots, and anything else they might need. They came ready to transform the wilderness into a "city on a hill," a visible example of true Christian faith.[6] The Puritans did not leave England because they believed in freedom of religion for everybody. They believed their own religion should be the one by which everyone worshipped.

The new settlers struggled but survived. They thrived by the thick woods, quick-rushing streams, and abundant open land. Soon, others joined them. By 1633, there were more than three thousand people living in an area called Massachusetts Bay Colony.

". . . the Easiest Room in Hell"

Religion took up much of the Puritans' time and energy. Puritans were required to attend three hours of church services each Sunday morning, and another two the same afternoon. Congregation members then went home and spent the rest of the day in prayer. On Thursdays, they gathered at the town's meetinghouse for an afternoon lecture.

During these long sermons, ministers threatened congregations with hellfire and damnation. They preached about the worthlessness of humankind. "Every man is born stark dead in sin," said minister Thomas Shepherd.[7] People were so wicked that good works alone could not save them. They could only pray for the grace of God to be merciful to undeserving sinners.

For Puritans in America, even a walk to church required a weapon for protection against Indians or wild animals.

Self-expression, self-assertion, or opposition to the community were signs of sin. Secular joy was discouraged and could be punished. A man in 1656 was sentenced to two hours in the stocks for "lewd and unseemly" behavior. He was forced to have his legs locked into a wooden frame, where neighbors could throw rotten fruits, eggs, and vegetables at him. Why? Because he kissed his wife in public when he returned home after spending three years at sea.[8]

Anything could be considered a crime. Those found guilty could be whipped, branded, or worse. In 1631, Boston's General Court (legislature) ruled "that Philip Ralliffe shall be whipped, have his eares cut off, fined 40 pounds, and banished out of the limits of this

---

SOURCE DOCUMENT

BRIDGET, WIFE OF THOMAS OLIVER, PRESENTED FOR CALLING HER HUSBAND MANY OPPROBRIOUS NAMES, AS OLD ROGUE AND OLD DEVIL, ON LORD'S DAYS, WAS ORDERED TO STAND WITH HER HUSBAND, BACK TO BACK, ON A LECTURE DAY IN THE PUBLIC MARKET PLACE, BOTH GAGGED, FOR ABOUT AN HOUR, WITH A PAPER FASTENED TO EACH OF THEIR FOREHEADS UPON WHICH THEIR OFFENSE SHALL BE FAIRLY WRITTEN.[9]

—SALEM, JAN. 29, 1677/78

Even offenses that today seem trivial were punishable by public humiliation in Puritan times. This is the verdict in the case of a married couple brought to court for fighting.

Puritan offenders suffered punishment by having their head and hands put in the pillory or their feet in the stocks.

jurisdiction, for uttering malicious and scandalous speeches against the Government."[10]

Even children did not escape the wrath of the Puritan religion. Babies were born with original sin. From the age of two, they were told of their worthlessness. Ministers and other adults used threats and terror to force acceptable behavior. Children soon learned that their parents could not be a source of comfort. Parents were much more likely to whip their children than to hug them. Noted minister Increase Mather warned youngsters that if they died without repenting of their sins, "Better you had never been born. . . . Your godly parents will testify against you before the Son of God."[11]

Puritan children received constant lessons on death and damnation to throw fear into their hearts. Ministers and other adults took children on walks through cemeteries to see where other young children were buried. A child was "never too little to die, and never too young to go to hell," according to historian Ernest Caulfield.[12] Michael Wigglesworth in 1662 wrote a 224-stanza poem, "The Day of Doom," well known to Puritan children. The poem gave little hope to children who died before they could be baptized:

> *I do confess, yours is much less*
> *though every sin's a crime.*
> *A crime it is, therefore in bliss*
> *you may not hope to dwell.*
> *But unto you I shall allow*
> *the easiest room in hell.*[13]

Carrying out God's Will

Puritans felt only they were capable of carrying out God's will in the Massachusetts Bay Colony. They requested and received a charter from the English king. This charter allowed for strong home rule—the right of the colony to make many of its own decisions. The charter did not have the usual clause requiring board meetings to be held in London. Boston, not London, would be the Puritan capital.

The government was far from a total democracy. Even though clergy members were prohibited from holding government offices, ministers had strong influence in the communities. Only male church members could vote. Church membership was not open to everyone; fewer than 20 percent of the population were members. A man or woman had to be elected to church membership by other members. Anyone seeking admission had to satisfy ministers and members with his or her purity. Even among members, there were social ranks. People with higher social status were addressed as "Mr." or "Mrs." Those on a lower scale were called "Goodman" or "Goodwife."

Church attendance was required even for non-members, who had to pay for church services, even though they had no say in the church's operation. Since only members could vote, the church's voice became the government's voice.

Foreign Affairs

Puritans in the colony of Massachusetts enjoyed more self-government than any other colony in the world in the 1600s. But they continually worried about what was happening on the other side of the Atlantic Ocean. England's changing political situation meant that their own government was fragile.

If James I was unfriendly to the Puritans, his successor was downright hostile. Charles I increased criticism of religious dissenters. Many more Puritans decided to leave England.

Charles's opposition did not last long. He proved as unpopular with Englishmen as he was with Massachusetts Puritans. A civil war in the 1640s toppled Charles from the throne. A stern Puritan Parliament member named Oliver Cromwell took over.

When Cromwell assumed power, English Puritans stopped their migration to America. In fact, some Massachusetts Puritans returned to England. They hoped that this Puritan leader would lead England to religious glory. Puritans took heart when Cromwell turned Anglican (Church of England) churches over to Puritans and forbade Anglican clergy from preaching or teaching.

But their enthusiasm for Cromwell was cautious. Even though he was a Puritan, he tolerated religious groups such as Jews and Quakers. He suggested that Massachusetts Bay colonists resettle in Ireland or Jamaica, to promote Puritanism in those places. The Massachusetts General Court, wishing to keep its own colony strong, did not favor that idea.

Cromwell died in 1658. His son Richard succeeded him, but Richard was an incompetent ruler. Parliament called for a restoration of the monarchy. Another king, Charles II, ascended the throne in 1660.

The second Charles proved as unfriendly to Puritans as the first. Under his rule, Parliament passed laws barring Puritans from government positions. In 1662, he sent a letter ordering that church membership would no longer be a voting requirement. Even worse, he revoked the Massachusetts Bay charter in 1684.

Charles's move panicked the colonists. Without a charter, they had no legal right to rule Massachusetts.

The king promised only minor changes if the Puritans would sign a revised charter. However, he now had a major change in mind. Charles wished to appoint a royal governor to lead the colony.

This proposal caused a bitter dispute in Massachusetts. Some favored following the king's wishes. Others sought a compromise. A third group held out to continue the old charter.

"I hope there is not one Freeman in Boston that will dare to be guilty of so great a sin [as voting to give up the old charter]," wrote outspoken minister Increase Mather, the strongest advocate of the old charter.[14] In 1688, Mather left for England to persuade the government to retain the old charter. If anyone could argue a case well, it was Massachusetts' most renowned clergyman.

Increase and Cotton

In a land where God's word was everything, ministers were the dominant personalities. A father and son, Increase and Cotton Mather, became the most influential ministers in Massachusetts Bay Colony.

Increase, son of noted minister Richard Mather, preached his first sermon at age eighteen. His fiery style inspired his congregations to follow Puritan values. Fear, not love, was the main message of his sermons. In 1674, he predicted that God would strike New England with his sword for its wickedness.

Cotton Mather, born in 1663, was considered even more brilliant than his father. He entered Harvard at age eleven. Cotton understood Greek, Latin, Spanish, and Iroquois, among other languages. He published fourteen books in one year. Cotton idolized his father and surpassed Increase's Puritan zeal. Cotton felt his soul was a major battleground in the war between God and Satan. He must uphold Puritan values to save God in New England.

"An Enchanted Universe"

"The people of seventeenth-century New England lived in an enchanted universe," noted historian David Hall. "Theirs was a world of wonders."[15] Another historian, George Lyman Kittredge, commented, "Our forefathers believed in witchcraft, not because they were Puritans, not because they were Colonials . . . but because they were men of their time."[16]

Lines blurred between the real and supernatural worlds. Magic was a very real part of religion. A 1686 comet was not seen as a celestial body orbiting the sun. Increase Mather called it "Heaven's Alarm to the World."[17]

To Puritans, the devil was a very real creature. Puritans believed that New England had been ruled by the devil until they arrived there. The devil was attacking his enemies. Any deviation from piety by the Puritans was a victory for Satan. Cotton Mather explained hard times by saying, "Where will the Devil show the most malice but where he is hated, and hateth most?"[18]

Witches were Satan's willing servants. The Mathers linked witchcraft, even "white" witchcraft, with Satan.

"Witchcraft, what shall I say of it?" Cotton Mather said. "It is the furthest effort of our original sin."[19]

Witchcraft, or accusations of it, could take many forms. Often they centered on unpopular community members, especially women. Ann Hibbens, an intelligent and outspoken widow, challenged local religious views in the 1650s. Her opinions alone did not damage her. But two neighbors also claimed she engaged in supernatural activities. Her case went all the way to the General Court. She was found guilty and executed in 1656. One of her defenders, minister John Norton, claimed she had been "hanged for a witch, only for having more wit than her neighbors."[20]

In 1688, Boston minister John Goodwin's children began acting strangely. They refused to eat, lost their hearing, and rolled wildly around the floor. Cotton Mather prayed over them, but their ailments continued.

A washerwoman, the widow Glover, was blamed for the children's behavior. Earlier, the children had claimed that she had stolen some of their clothes. The widow cursed the children for making the accusation. Cotton Mather called Glover "an ignorant and scandalous old Woman."[21] The widow confessed to witchcraft, saying she squeezed puppets to cast spells. She was sentenced to death and executed.

Puritan Problems

Earthly as well as supernatural problems dogged the Puritans in the late 1600s. Their relationship with American Indians, once cordial, soured. They nearly

Ann Hibbens, an intelligent and outspoken widow, was hanged for challenging local religious views in 1656.

exterminated the Pequot tribe in 1637. Most of the Pequot who survived were sold into slavery. King Philip, a Massasoit chief, tried to drive away the white settlers in 1675. The bloody conflict known as King Philip's War killed one tenth of the Massachusetts Bay colonists. It turned out to be even more costly for the Indians. About twenty-five hundred of the three thousand warriors were either killed or sold into slavery.

Events in England also made the Puritans uneasy. James II, who succeeded Charles II in 1685, sent Sir Edmund Andros to rule the New England colony in 1686. New Englanders hated the royal governor, with good reason. He established an Anglican Church in Boston, which ended the Puritans' religious monopoly there. Andros also abolished the lower house of the legislature, imposed new taxes, and arrested those who would not cooperate with him.

James II was Catholic, and his wife gave birth to a son in 1688. English Protestants feared a Catholic monarchy might mean the end of their religious freedom. They enlisted William of Orange, a Dutchman, to overthrow James. William and his wife, Mary, took the English throne after a bloodless 1688 coup known as the Glorious Revolution.

Puritans, following the example of the Glorious Revolution, imprisoned Andros in 1689. It was a hollow victory. They no longer had a despised governor, but now they had no government at all.

The new rulers, by their religious tolerance, proved to be as much a threat to the Puritans as James. They excluded Jews and Catholics from government office, but gave religious freedom to all Protestants. This meant that Church of England members, as well as Puritans, could practice their faith.

William and Mary's rule posed a threat for another reason. The new English leaders sought to oust the French from North America. The French, allied with various Indian groups, attacked New England's northern regions. New Englanders, under the leadership of Sir William Phips, tried to stop the French by attacking Quebec City. The 1690 invasion attempt failed miserably. Refugees from northern regions streamed into the Massachusetts Bay Colony.

Factors even greater than governments and wars were upsetting the Puritans. Changes were overcoming the Western world. These changes were greater than anything a group of religious purists could challenge. Money was replacing religion as a major social influence. Overseas commerce made New Englanders aware of other countries and new ideas.

These ideas included scientific discoveries. By the end of the seventeenth century, modern science was taking a foothold in Europe. Sir Isaac Newton published *Principia Matematica* in 1687, which is still considered a basis for scientific study.

New England, however, did not leap to embrace all modern ideas. Cotton Mather published a book in 1689 called *Memorable Provinces Relating to Witchcraft and Possessions*. He used the book to try to explain the devil and witchcraft in scientific terms. It became a best-seller in New England.

Crises abounded in New England at the end of the seventeenth century. There were potential conflicts with the French and American Indians. The government was unstable. Those with a more worldly view disagreed with strictly Puritan ideas. Diseases such as smallpox crippled the population. The extremely cold winter of 1691 to 1692 caused further damage. Nowhere were all these factors more evident than in the small farm settlement known as Salem Village.

4

"NEIGHBORS AGAINST NEIGHBORS"

It appeared to be a perfect location, with a fine natural harbor and rivers leading inland. The Puritans named the coastal town Salem, from the Hebrew word *shalom*, meaning "peace." From the beginning, the town thrived. It prospered so much that soon all nearby land on the coast was taken. Newcomers would have to move inland.

They did move, five to ten miles west of Salem Town. By the 1660s, a scattered collection of farms had appeared. This area became known as Salem Village.

Town versus Village

Salem Town and Salem Village shared a name, but not much else. From the start, their ways of life differed greatly. Salem Town became a thriving fishing town and trading center. Salem Town and Boston were the major ports of the Massachusetts Bay Colony. Merchants from the town traveled throughout Europe, Asia, Africa, and the Americas. They collected goods and ideas from the people they visited, then returned to their fine homes.

Salem Village, on the other hand, was little more than a frontier settlement. Bears, wolves, and wildcats posed a constant threat to settlers and livestock. To the north and west lay forests. Indians in those forest lands were not always friendly. Salem Town was hours away over muddy, dusty, or icy roads. Boston, the capital, was twenty-eight miles distant. It took more than a day for Salem villagers to travel there.

Salem townspeople were worldly. Salem villagers were farmers. "Education was generally neglected [in Salem Village]," noted historian Edward Eggleston. "Even men of substance were sometimes unable to write."[1]

Salem villagers resented the government control Salem Town held over them. Almost from the beginning, the Salem Village farmers wanted independence from the town. Salem Town, however, had no intention of surrendering control of the village. Other towns—Wenham, Manchester, and Beverly—had already broken away from Salem Town. Salem Village could provide food and tax revenue; townspeople saw no reason to let it go.

Villagers especially resented nighttime guard duty. They, along with town members, were required to take turns on a night watch for the town. Villagers felt cheated. They were in greater danger from Indian raids than were town members. Yet town members did not help guard their property. In 1667, villagers petitioned the court to exempt themselves from military duty, "considering how remote our dwellings are from

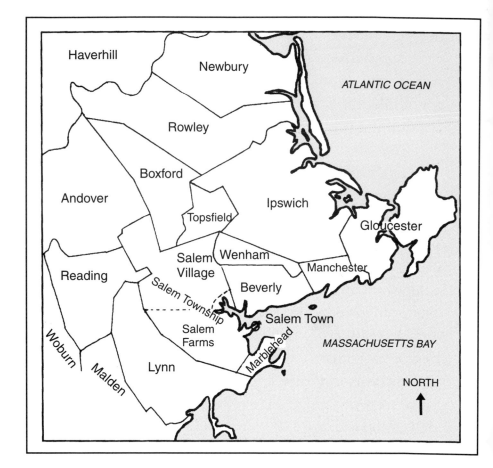

Salem Town and adjacent Salem Village shared a name, but little else. The town became a fishing and trading center. The village was mainly a farming community.

the town."[2] A court finally permitted those more than four miles from the Salem Town meetinghouse to skip the evening duty.

The resentment between Salem Village and Salem Town was more than just an economic or power matter. Many villagers feared and distrusted the social changes they saw in the town. They felt that Puritan social and religious values were eroding there. In their own village, they wished to keep those values intact.

Putnams versus Porters

Salem villagers might have felt resentment over their treatment by Salem town members. But they did not necessarily show brotherhood or sisterhood toward each other. Courts kept busy settling disputes between neighbors. Most often, these lawsuits involved disagreements over property. These were not petty arguments. "If there was a squabble over a small bit of land, it could make a difference between a comfortable and a cold winter," said historian Richard Trask.[3]

By the late 1670s, Salem Village was known for its internal discord. Resident Jeremiah Watts described the village as "brother against brother and neighbors against neighbors, all quarreling and smiting one another."[4] The most important feud involved Salem Village's two leading families, the Putnams and the Porters.

John Putnam and John Porter both came to Salem in the early 1640s. Both soon moved to the Salem Village area. John Putnam had three adult sons:

Thomas, Nathaniel, and John. Porter's three surviving sons—Joseph, Benjamin, and Israel—were all younger than the Putnam offspring.

Both families prospered, especially the Porters. John Putnam's farm was eight hundred acres, but John Porter had nearly two thousand acres when he died in 1676. Their means of livelihood differed. The Porters lived in the eastern region of Salem Village, closer to the town. They identified with the town's commercial interests and were active in town affairs. The Putnams lived on the more remote western side. They were farmers. They held more strongly to the old ways of Puritanism than did the Porters. The Putnams, not the Porters, dominated village politics.

The Putnams invested their savings in more land. But after a while, available land ran out, and there were more and more Putnam mouths to feed. The Putnams and Porters had never enjoyed a cordial relationship. Unfriendliness would soon grow into open hostility.

As was customary, when John Putnam died, his oldest son, Thomas, received the largest share of his estate. Thomas and his first wife had three sons. After his wife died, Thomas married a woman named Mary Veren. They had a son, Joseph.

When Thomas died in 1686, his oldest son, Thomas, Jr., did not get most of the estate. Instead, wife Mary and youngest son Joseph got nearly all of it. Furthermore, Thomas, Sr., had written in his will that Joseph would inherit the money at age eighteen, not the usual age of twenty-one. Brothers Thomas and

Edward and brothers-in-law Jonathan Walcott and William Trask went to court to contest the will. The court, however, upheld it. Joseph Putnam, not even twenty-one years old, was now the second richest person in Salem Village.

Soon afterward, Joseph married the daughter of the powerful Salem villager, Putnam-family foe Israel Porter. Joseph was now a Putnam in name only.

The Porter family fortune was now growing, while the Putnams suffered. When he died in 1686, the elder Thomas Putnam was the wealthiest man in Salem Village. Ten years later, his son Thomas was only the sixteenth richest.

Putnams continued to battle with the Porters. Soon this feud would move into an unlikely arena—Salem's meetinghouse.

Church Wars

Puritans did not believe in elaborate churches. Instead, they had unadorned meetinghouses. Every Sunday and Thursday, local residents gathered to hear God's word. At times the meetinghouse served other purposes as well. Important trials or government sessions could be held there.

Salem villagers lacked an organized church. They did not even have a meetinghouse. Villagers had to make a lengthy trip to Salem Town for church services. Uncertain weather and poor roads made these trips uncomfortable, even hazardous.

In 1666, Salem Village residents asked the town's

council for permission to hire a minister of their own because of "great distance from the meetinghouse."[5] The council refused. The villagers took their request all the way to the General Court. Six years later, after pressure from the General Court, the Salem Town council permitted the village to build a church. The town allowed the village to be exempt from town church taxes. However, it stressed that the village must pay other town taxes.

Villagers wasted no time in hiring a minister. James Bayley came to the village in 1672. From the start, there was trouble. The village gave him land. It had voted to build him a house but did not do so. Some villagers refused to pay taxes for the church.

Continual disputes among villagers made Bayley's term a nightmare. In 1679, a minority group led by Nathaniel Putnam called for Bayley's ouster. A debate continued for months. It seemed to center less on Bayley's skills than on which faction had the power to hire or fire a minister. By November of that year, Putnam had enough votes to remove Bayley. The besieged minister resigned, moved to Connecticut, and never returned to Salem Village.

In 1680, Salem Village found another minister. George Burroughs had served a congregation in the Maine wilderness. He fled to Massachusetts in 1676 during King Philip's War. Burroughs hoped to calm the quarrelsome village. As a condition of his employment, he requested "that in case any difference shall arise in time to come, that we engage on both sides to submit to counsel for a peaceable issue."[6]

Burroughs was no more successful at keeping peace than was Bayley. Before the Salem Village parsonage was built in 1680, Burroughs and his wife stayed with John Putnam and his wife. For whatever reason, they did not get along. This unfriendliness spread through much of the congregation.

By 1683, some villagers had refused to pay their minister. Burroughs was not receiving his full salary. In March, he stopped serving the congregation. He resigned from the Salem Village ministry and returned to Maine.

Villagers invited Burroughs to return that May. He might have thought he would get the £33 (roughly $33,000 in today's money) that was due to him. However, John Putnam called upon the local marshal to arrest Burroughs and throw him into jail. Putnam charged that Burroughs had never repaid him £6 for funeral wine following the minister's wife's death.

Burroughs received his back wages and paid off local debts. Then he went off to Casco, Maine. No doubt he hoped he would never see this wretched village again.

Another minister, Deodat Lawson, came in 1684. He fell prey to village politics. Neither previous minister had ever been formally ordained. This meant they could not serve communion or perform some other religious functions. One Salem Village faction, led by John Putnam and Thomas Putnam, Jr., wanted to

SOURCE DOCUMENT

THE LORD DOTH TERRIBLE THINGS AMONGST US, BY LENGTHENING THE CHAIN OF THE ROARING LION IN AN EXTRAORDINARY MANNER, SO THAT THE DEVIL IS COME DOWN IN GREAT WRATH . . . ENDEAVORING TO SET UP HIS KINGDOM, AND BY RACKING TORMENTS ON BODIES, AND AFFRIGHTENING REPRESENTATIONS TO THE MIND OF MANY AMONGST US. . . . [7]

Deodat Lawson preached typical Puritan sermons, such as "Christ's Fidelity the Only Shield Against Satan's Malignity," which frightened Puritans by describing the devil's wrath.

create a full-fledged church, with Lawson as an ordained minister.

Joseph Porter and brother-in-law Daniel Andrew, allied with Salem Town interests, opposed such a move. Their friend Joseph Hutchinson made his opposition known in a direct fashion. Hutchinson had given the village land in 1673 for a meetinghouse site. Now he reclaimed the land and put a fence around it.

Villagers could not agree on the ordination issue. They called a five-man arbitration board to decide it. The board advised against the ordination until both sides could cool their tempers. They commented that if the local animosity were not prevented, it "will let out peace and order and let in confusion and every evil work."[8] The words proved prophetic.

Lawson's contract ended in 1688. He wasted no time in departing from Salem Village. Now villagers were becoming desperate. Three ministers had left on bad terms in less than ten years. A first-rate candidate was out of the question. Who in his right mind would want to tend this strife-torn community?

But they needed somebody who would come in and be minister to a Salem Village church. In the spring of 1689, they found their person.

Samuel Parris

Samuel Parris was a failure at everything he had tried. He had attended Harvard College, the colony's seminary, but never graduated. When his father died, he inherited some land in Barbados. A 1678 hurricane ravaged that land.

Parris moved to Boston in early 1681. He purchased a wharf and warehouse there. That business proved less than successful. Parris then gave up being a merchant and entered the ministry.

Now here he was at age thirty-six, not a wealthy businessman, not a respected Boston clergyman. Instead, he was forced to accept a job in a backwater village that had a reputation for internal disharmony.

Samuel Parris retained his business instincts, however. A group of Salem villagers approached him in 1689. They offered sixty pounds annually—one third in salary, the rest in corn and other goods.

Parris made a counteroffer. He wanted a higher salary, a raise in pay if money became more plentiful, and free firewood. Most important, he wanted a house. Villagers had offered to let him use the village minister's house, rent-free. Parris, perhaps knowing of the problems Lawson had suffered with Joseph Hutchinson, wanted more security. He demanded that the house be deeded to him and his heirs. A faction led by the Putnam family agreed to the demand.

This house agreement enraged other villagers. Joseph Hutchinson had donated land to the village on the condition that it not be given away. Parris now had a house, but he also gained the dislike and distrust of many of Salem Village's residents.

Parris's foes struck back. They refused to gather firewood for him, claiming that money for wood was included in his salary. Many of them also refused to contribute to his salary. Parris denounced them as "knaves and cheaters."[9]

By late 1691, they had the upper hand. Five Parris opponents won the election for the village council that fall. The friendly faces of John and Nathaniel Putnam were no longer in charge. Parris now faced a government headed by Joseph Porter, Joseph Putnam, Joseph Hutchinson, Daniel Andrew, and Francis Nurse. This new group voted that no money should be raised to pay Parris's salary.

Parris still had his allies—the governing members of the church. In November, they formally asked the village council to levy a tax to pay the minister's salary. When the council did not respond, the church sued it in court.

Anti-Parris forces fought back. On December 1, the new council called for a special meeting. This group sought to overturn the previous council ruling that had given Parris the parsonage. Nothing came of the threat. Parris kept the house, but the church withdrew the lawsuit.

These legal maneuvers only made Parris angrier. His sermons now frequently contained thinly veiled criticisms of his foes.

The long-stirring conflicts in Salem Village were now coming to a head. It would take only a small spark to ignite an open outbreak of hatred. That spark came from a most unlikely source—a slave from the West Indies named Tituba.

5

"SUSPICION OF WITCHCRAFT"

Even by New England standards, the winter of 1691–1692 was a cruel one. Residents battled some of the coldest temperatures the colony had ever seen. Snowstorms and ice made travel difficult, if not impossible. Epidemics of smallpox ravaged Massachusetts. King William's War, being fought by Great Britian and its American colonies against the French and their Indian allies, had continued for more than three years. New Englanders worried about attacks by the French and Indians. There was little to do but stay inside.

During the best of times, life was confining for young girls in New England. Boys could hunt, fish, and explore the countryside. Girls, however, were expected to stay home and tend the house. And these were not the best of times.

"A Specter in Likeness of a Coffin"

Betty Parris and Abigail Williams were two such New England girls. Betty was the nine-year-old daughter of the minister, Samuel Parris. Abigail, eleven, probably an orphan, was his niece. Fortunately, they had a source of entertainment in their home. Tituba, a slave Parris had brought from Barbados, talked with them on these winter nights. She entertained them with imaginative tales of fairies and supernatural spirits.

Sometimes, other girls joined them. There was Ann Putnam, the twelve-year-old daughter of leading citizen Thomas Putnam. Mercy Lewis, the Putnams' nineteen-year-old servant, also came along. Elizabeth Hubbard, the seventeen-year-old niece of Dr. William Griggs, sometimes showed up. So did Mary Walcott, sixteen, daughter of Putnam in-law Jonathan Walcott. Twenty-year-old Mary Warren, the servant of tavern keeper John Proctor, occasionally visited.

The girls did more than listen to stories. Sometimes they played fortune-telling games. Samuel Parris would have been furious if he had known of these games. To him, fortune-telling meant associating with the devil. But the girls wanted to know their future. Who would they marry? Would their lives be happy?

One day, one of the girls dropped the white of a raw egg into a glass. The shape of its blob was supposed to predict the future. The blob became "a specter in likeness of a coffin."[1] That meant someone was going to die.

Witch Cake

Betty Parris, more than the others, grew up with the fear of sin. Her fanatical father viewed everything as either completely good or totally evil. Perhaps guilt or anxiety from playing sinful fortune-telling games affected her. For whatever reason, in late December 1691, she began to act strangely. She complained of knifelike pains throughout her body. She experienced temporary loss of speech, sight, hearing, and appetite. Betty had sudden fits of weeping. She became absent-minded and forgot to do chores.

Elizabeth Hubbard's uncle, Dr. Griggs, examined Betty. He found no physical reason for her illness. Griggs became convinced that there could be only one explanation for Betty's problems: The girl was a victim of witchcraft.

Mary Sibley, a neighbor, tried to help the girl. She told Tituba and her husband, a man known as John

SOURCE DOCUMENT

DIVERS[E] YOUNG PERSONS BELONGING TO MR. PARRIS' FAMILY, AND ONE OR MORE OF THE NEIGHBOURHOOD, BEGAN TO ACT, AFTER A STRANGE AND UNUSUAL MANNER, VIZ/ AS BY GETTING INTO HOLES, AND CREEPING UNDER CHAIRS AND STOOLS, AND TO USE SUNDRY ODD POSTURES AND ANTIC GESTURES, UTTERING FOOLISH, RIDICULOUS SPEECHES, WHICH NEITHER THEY THEMSELVES NOR ANY OTHERS COULD MAKE SENSE OF; THE PHYSICIANS THAT WERE CALLED . . . TOLD THEM HE WAS AFRAID THEY WERE BEWITCHED. . . .[2]

In late 1691 and early 1692, unexplained behavior by Betty Parris, Abigail Williams, and others led to charges of witchcraft against residents of Salem Village and nearby communities.

Indian, to make a witch cake. They were to make a cake from flour and Betty's urine, then feed it to a dog. The dog, bewitched by the cake, would reveal the witch's name. Tituba knew nothing of this English superstition but gave it a try anyway.

The witch cake cured nothing. Instead, the affliction spread to other girls. Abigail Williams made babbling sounds and crawled on all fours like a dog. Ann Putnam, Elizabeth Hubbard, Mercy Lewis, and Mary Walcott also showed bizarre symptoms.

Parris had to do something. His daughter showed no signs of improvement. Besides, it was a disgrace for the devil to have a foothold in *his* house. Betty and the others would have to cry out and accuse those who were harming them. Finally, in late February 1692, Betty gave the reason for her illness. She was bewitched by three persons: Sarah Good, Sarah Osborne, and Tituba.

The Beggar, the Invalid, and the Slave

Puritans did not believe that all men and women were equal before God. They certainly did not believe that all humans were equal on earth. The three women Betty Parris accused of witchcraft represented the low end of the local Puritan social ladder.

Life had not always been hard for Sarah Good. Her father, John Solart, was a respectable farmer. But he had drowned himself in 1672, when Sarah was nineteen. Her mother had remarried, and Sarah's stepfather had tried to cheat Sarah out of the inheritance left to her by her father.

Things only got worse. Sarah married a poor indentured servant. When he died, she was left with debts. Later she married a laborer, William Good. A lawsuit forced them to sell off their property. By 1692, Sarah Good had become a homeless, sharp-tongued, thirty-eight-year-old pregnant beggar, smoking her ever-present pipe and seeking food for herself and her daughter. She said she had not attended church "for want of clothes."[3]

Her attitude bothered villagers as much as her poverty. Instead of accepting her bad fortune as God's will, she appeared to be resentful of it. When neighbors refused to help her, she sometimes muttered at them. Some took these mutterings to be curses. After all, she had scowled at a neighbor a few years before. Soon afterward, the neighbor's livestock died.

Sarah Osborne lacked Sarah Good's sour temperament. Even so, she was less than highly regarded in the community. When her first husband died, his will gave land to their children. Sarah and her new husband Alexander Osborne fought the will, hoping to get the land for themselves. This was particularly scandalous to the Putnam family. Sarah Osborne's first husband had been Robert Prince, whose sister was married to John Putnam, Sr. Thus, Sarah's action was robbing land from the extended Putnam family.

Sarah Osborne was controversial in other ways. Rumors said she had lived with Osborne before marrying him, a major sin for Puritans. Like Sarah Good, Sarah Osborne had not been going to church. She was too old and ill to attend.

Even though Samuel Parris was a man of God, he saw no harm in owning slaves. His slave Tituba and her husband, John Indian, came with him from Barbados. Tituba helped around the house. John Indian worked part-time in the tavern of Parris's ally, Samuel Ingersoll.

Since Tituba was considered Parris's property, he could do with her what he liked. He sometimes beat her to get her to follow his wishes. To escape his beatings, Tituba would say whatever she thought Parris wanted to hear.

By all accounts, Sarah Good, Sarah Osborne, and Tituba were not friends. They might not have even known each other. But on February 29, 1692, their lives became linked. On that day Thomas and Edward Putnam and two others appeared before Salem Town magistrates John Hathorne and Jonathan Corwin. They asked for and got arrest warrants against the women for "suspicion of witchcraft."[4] The following day, all three women were arrested.

"The Devil . . . Bid Me Serve Him"

On March 1, John Hathorne and Jonathan Corwin rode from bustling Salem Town to sleepy Salem Village. A surprise awaited them at the farm settlement. People from miles around had crowded into Ingersoll's tavern to see the examination of the suspected witches.

The proceedings had to be moved to the meetinghouse to hold the throng of interested spectators.

This examination was part of the legal process. First, someone had to file a complaint. Then, magistrates would hold a hearing to investigate the charge. If there appeared to be sufficient evidence, the accused would be thrown into jail to await a grand jury's action. If the grand jury indicted the accused, a trial before a jury of landowners would determine innocence or guilt.

Hathorne and Corwin, both respected businessmen in Salem Town, would serve as magistrates, though neither had legal experience. Hathorne assured his friend Thomas Putnam that he would do what was necessary to bring the witches to justice.

From the beginning, the outcome of the examinations was never in doubt. Hathorne presumed the accused women guilty. His questions took the form of accusations. Corwin went along with him.

They even showed their prejudice in the handling of the courtroom decorum. Courts are generally quiet places where the quiet of the room represents the importance of the situation. But the meetinghouse at Salem sometimes suggested an insane asylum more than a court of law. Betty Parris, Abigail Williams, Ann Putnam, and other girls who claimed to be afflicted by witchcraft sat in the front row. Shocked spectators watched as the girls screamed and wriggled on the floor when the accused women spoke. Neither magistrate did anything to stop the girls' odd behavior.

Dozens of suspected witches awaited trial inside Salem's Old Witch Jail.

Sarah Good was the first accused woman called to testify. She maintained her innocence. After all, what proof did anyone have of her guilt? She carried no dolls or puppets with which to cast spells. No one ever saw her commit a supernatural act. She had no body marks that could be seen as witches' teats. The girls would not accept her pleas of innocence. They claimed that her specter was pinching them. Sarah Good said she did nothing. It must be Sarah Osborne who was bothering the afflicted girls.

The luckless Sarah Good stood little chance. Even her husband William spoke against her. He told the magistrates that he was afraid "that either she was a witch, or would be one very quickly."[5] Perhaps more important, the girls charged that Sarah Good's spirit, not her body, was harming them. The magistrates were willing to accept the girls' spectral evidence. Sarah Good's position was hopeless. How could she prove that a spirit was or was not doing something?

Sarah Osborne, like Sarah Good, denied guilt. She claimed that she was a witchcraft victim, not a witch. When the afflicted girls looked at her, she began shrieking and shaking. Her actions, however, failed to convince the magistrates.

When Osborne left, Tituba entered the room. At first, screams and shouts greeted her appearance. Once she began speaking, the room fell to a deathlike hush. Unlike Sarah Good and Sarah Osborne, the West

SOURCE DOCUMENT

I HAVE VERY OFTEN BEEN MOST GRIEVOUSLY TORTURED BY [THE] APPARITION OF SARAH GOOD, WHO HAS THE MOST DREADFULLY AFFLICTED ME BY BITING, PRICKING, AND PINCHING ME, AND ALMOST CHOKING ME TO DEATH. BUT ON THE 26 JUNE, 1692, SARAH GOOD MOST VIOLENTLY PULLED DOWN MY HEAD BEHIND A CHEST AND TIED MY HANDS TOGETHER WITH A WHALE BAND, AND ALMOST CHOKED ME TO DEATH.[6]

Susannah Sheldon testified in the trial against Sarah Good that Good's specter had violently attacked her.

Indian woman did not deny witchcraft. In fact, she made a major confession.

For five days, spectators listened rapt to Tituba's fantastic testimony. She told incredible tales of local witches and witchcraft. She said strange creatures threatened to harm her if she did not harm Betty and the other girls. Tituba told of red rats, talking cats, hairy imps, and people flying through the sky on poles. She claimed that a tall man dressed in black (obviously the devil) asked her to make her mark in a book. She said Sarah Good and Sarah Osborne had signed the book, too. "The Devil came to me and bid me serve him," she claimed.[7] Sometimes the devil came to her with Sarah Good, Sarah Osborne, and two other women whom she did not recognize.

Tituba's testimony, although fascinating, added no solid evidence to the proceedings. The only women she named had already been accused by the afflicted girls. Most likely, she said what she thought would please Samuel Parris.

One important person escaped questioning. Mary Sibley had advised Tituba to make a witch cake. Surely that would qualify as witchcraft. Yet Samuel Parris spoke on her behalf. He claimed he had met with her, and she confessed her sin. Mary Sibley was never charged with witchcraft.

Sarah Good, Sarah Osborne, and Tituba were not so fortunate. Off they went to the Boston jail until a trial could be arranged. Had there been opposition to the women's imprisonment, there might not have been further arrests. But the women's neighbors made no protest.

Betty Parris also left Salem Village. Her father sent her to live with one of his friends, Captain Stephen Sewall, in Salem Town. Away from the turmoil of Salem Village, she soon recovered her health.

For the rest of Salem's villagers, however, the terror was only beginning.

The arrest of the three women did nothing to cure the girls' ills. If anything, their condition became worse. Minister John Hale of Beverly commented that the girls' movements were "beyond the power of any epileptic fits, or natural disease to effect."[1]

"THESE FOLKS THAT ARE OUT OF THEIR WITS"

"Whish! Whish!"

Reverend Samuel Parris now sought the advice of other ministers. Parris invited former local minister Deodat Lawson to visit Salem Village. Lawson had barely arrived at Ingersoll's tavern when someone knocked on his door. It was Mary Walcott, Jonathan Walcott's daughter. She suddenly screamed that someone was biting her. A moment later, Lawson "saw apparently the marks of teeth, both upper and lower, on each side of her wrist."[2]

The next day, Lawson visited the parsonage. As he was talking with Samuel Parris, Abigail Williams came into the room, flapping her arms and shouting "Whish! Whish!"[3] A moment later, she shouted that

Rebecca Nurse's specter was trying to force her to sign the forbidden book. Then she ran into the fireplace and tried to climb up the chimney.

When Lawson preached a sermon that Sunday, some of the girls shouted and interrupted him. This behavior was unbelievable for Puritan children. Lawson returned to Boston and spread the word: Witchcraft had taken over Salem Village.

Gospel Women

Meanwhile, the afflicted girls and women continued their accusations. But now the accused persons represented a different social group. The first three women charged as witches were outcasts in Salem Village—a slave, an ill-tempered homeless beggar, and an old woman who disturbed social customs by not attending church. Martha Corey fit none of those descriptions.

Salem villagers recognized Martha Corey as an upright, churchgoing woman. But sixty-five-year-old Corey was an independent thinker who had more than a bit of a temper. Her husband Giles decided to go to Salem Village to watch the examinations of the first accused women. Martha tried to stop him by removing the saddle from his horse.

The elderly Corey considered herself a "gospel woman."[4] When Edward Putnam visited her before her arrest, Corey laughed. She said "I do not think [the women in prison] are witches."[5] Corey added, "You have no reason to think so of me, for I have made a

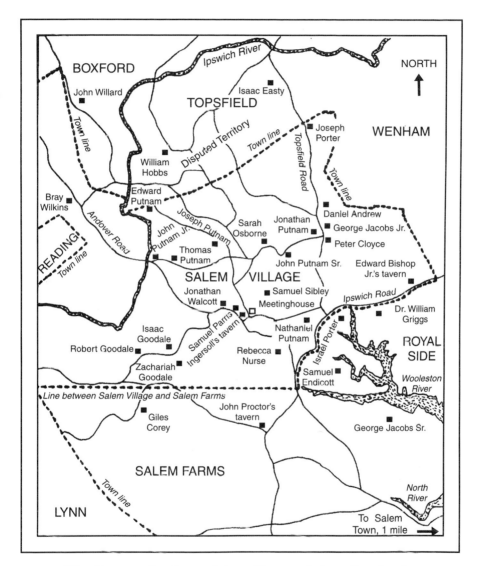

The Putnam family and its allies tended to live in the western portion of Salem Village, while opponents, including many of those accused of witchcraft, tended to live in the east, nearer Salem Town.

profession of Christ and have rejoiced to go and hear the word of God."[6]

Martha Corey went to the house of Ann Putnam, Sr., Ann's mother. The elder Ann was Corey's accuser. One observer noted "no sonner [sooner] did martha Corey Come into the hous[e] of thomas putnam but ann putnam fell into grevious feets [fits] of Choking[,] blinding[,] feat and hands twisted in a most grevious man[n]er."[7]

A warrant for Martha Corey's arrest was issued on Saturday, March 19, 1692. However, she could not be picked up until the following Monday. Meanwhile, Corey attended church services at the meetinghouse that Sunday. Some felt her attendance was an act of open defiance. They were further shocked when Abigail Williams screamed that she saw a yellow bird, a familiar, near Martha Corey.

The Monday examination opened with a prayer by Nicholas Noyes. Corey then asked to be allowed to pray. The magistrates denied her request. Magistrate Hathorne asked her if the girls were bewitched. She responded, "They might be for aught I know. I have no hand in it."[8] Such apparent disrespect did her little good. Her husband, Giles Corey, was no help. He claimed that his wife disturbed his prayers. Martha Corey ended up in prison with Sarah Good, Sarah Osborne, and Tituba.

The next arrest was even more shocking. Rebecca Nurse had a well-known reputation for goodness. At least, the seventy-one-year-old human body of Rebecca

Nurse enjoyed such a reputation. Her specter, according to the afflicted girls, led a very different existence. This spirit, supposedly unseen to all but the afflicted girls, tried to do the devil's work.

Nurse told the magistrates, "I can say before my eternal father that I am innocent, and God will clear my innocence." Hathorne knew of her lifetime of church service. He responded, "Here is never a one in the assembly but desires it."[9] However, he told her, "You would do well if you were guilty to confess." Rebecca Nurse could do no such thing. That would be a lie, a major sin in the eyes of God. "Would you have me belie myself?" she asked the magistrate.[10]

Protests of innocence did not help her. When Nurse testified, the girls reacted wildly. If she shook her head to one side, Elizabeth Hubbard moved her neck in the same direction. If she leaned back, the girls leaned far back, too. Her friends and family presented a petition to Hathorne. Even John Putnam, Sr., and his grandson Jonathan Putnam signed it. Hathorne's sister, Elizabeth Porter, spoke out on Nurse's behalf. Nevertheless, Rebecca Nurse ended up in jail.

She got no pity from the local minister. Samuel Parris preached a sermon in early April. Its title was "Christ Knows How Many Devils There Are in His Church, and Who They Are." Many, including Sarah Cloyce, Rebecca Nurse's sister, thought he was referring to Nurse. Cloyce stood up in the middle of the sermon, walked out of the meetinghouse, and slammed the door behind her. An openmouthed congregation could not believe this protest.

From Children to Elders

Martha Corey and Rebecca Nurse were not the only ones arrested. Soon a stream of accused witches of all ages flowed into the meetinghouse to await the magistrates' decisions. By now, a pattern was emerging. Ann Putnam, Jr., was usually the first afflicted person to cry out on someone. Then, she was joined by others: Abigail Williams, Elizabeth Hubbard, Mercy Lewis, and Mary Walcott. John Indian, Tituba's husband, occasionally joined this group. He saw his wife, an accused witch, in jail while the afflicted girls were running free. It appeared obvious that it was safer for him to pretend to be afflicted rather than risk being accused. Ann Putnam, Sr., who some believe showed signs of mental instability even before the girls' illness, sometimes cried out with the afflicted girls. After the afflicted persons cried out, someone issued a formal complaint. This was often Thomas, Edward, or Jonathan Putnam, or Thomas Putnam's brother-in-law, Jonathan Walcott.

Among those taken into custody as a witch was Dorcas Good, Sarah Good's five-year-old daughter. Like the others, she was sent to jail. She was described as "a hale [healthy] and well-looking girl" when imprisoned.[11] Her little hands and feet were too small to be held by the jail's chains. Special manacles had to be made for her.

Mary Easty, sister of Rebecca Nurse and Sarah Cloyce, also came before the magistrates. Like her sisters, she was a respected church member. Hathorne turned to the girls and asked, "Are you sure this is the woman?"[12] When they turned their heads grotesquely, Hathorne ordered Mary Easty to prison. When she was released a few weeks later, the girls went into severe fits. Easty was rearrested.

Salem villagers knew Abigail Hobbs as a rebel. She once claimed she had made a pact with the devil and had sold herself "body and soul to the Old Boy."[13] She might have wanted the respect and attention that the afflicted girls enjoyed. But the afflicted girls came from the village's most respected families. Hobbs's lower-class background kept her from this inner circle. Even though she cried out against others, she did not escape prison.

Nehemiah Abbott also appeared before Hathorne and Corwin. He lived in neighboring Topsfield, not Salem Village, but one of the girls cried out on him anyway. When he came to the examination, most of the girls did not recognize him. The magistrates released him. He became the only person to be freed during the examinations.

"Oh, You Are a Grievous Liar"!

Not everyone took the proceedings respectfully. Shortly after Sarah Cloyce walked out of the meetinghouse, John Indian cried out on her. When he accused her at the examination of hurting him, she responded,

"Oh, you are a grievous liar."[14] Martha Carrier, an accused woman known for speaking her mind, scolded Hathorne. Carrier pointed to the girls and told him, "It is a shameful thing that you should mind these folks that are out of their wits."[15]

John Proctor's servant, Mary Warren, also fell into fits. However, Proctor refused to tolerate her actions. He felt the afflicted girls were troublemakers who should be punished. He threatened to "thrash the devil out of her" unless she stopped her strange behavior.[16] For a time, the threat worked.

Although Mary Warren was silenced, others continued to complain. John Indian claimed that the specter of John Proctor's wife, Elizabeth, tried to choke him. The girls then joined in on the charges. When Proctor tried to defend his wife at the examination, the afflicted people accused him as well. After John and Elizabeth Proctor went to prison, Sheriff George Corwin, the magistrate's brother, seized their property.

Mary Warren, at first, refused to speak out against her mistress. Then, the other girls turned against Warren. They charged her with witchcraft, and she ended up in prison. After three weeks in captivity, the servant girl gave up. She denounced John Proctor and was freed shortly afterward.

Abigail Williams accused Elizabeth Cary of Charleston. Cary and her husband, Nathaniel, went to Salem Village to investigate the charges. Both believed there must be some mistake.

The Carys went to the meetinghouse during an examination. No one recognized them, even when they gave their names. There, they saw the magistrate order an accused person to touch an afflicted girl. Puritans believed that by touching an innocent, the witch would remove the spell from him or her. Nathaniel Cary questioned the process. He said, "As soon as they were touched by the accused, the justices would say, 'They are well,' before I could discern any alteration."[17]

Then they went to Ingersoll's tavern. John Indian, a waiter at the tavern, insisted on showing them scars he claimed came from witchcraft. They questioned whether anyone could take this man seriously.

The couple asked to meet in private with Abigail Williams. Instead, a group of the girls came into the tavern, rolled on the floor, and wailed. When they went to the meetinghouse, John Indian "fell down and tumbled about like a hog, but said nothing."[18] Nathaniel Cary was not permitted to speak in his wife's defense, and she was detained. After she went to prison, he arranged her escape. They fled to Rhode Island, then to New York.

Some of Massachusetts' most prominent people received summonses. One of them was Boston trader John Alden. His father had been one of the original *Mayflower* pilgrims. He had won fame as a soldier and an Indian fighter. Alden was tall. He might have fit the description of the tall man from Boston whom Tituba said tormented her.

John Alden showed no respect for the accusers. When he got to the meetinghouse, the girls did not recognize him. When a magistrate asked an afflicted girl to identify Alden, she pointed to the wrong man at first. Then, she selected Alden. When the magistrate asked her how she knew Alden was the right man, the girl answered, "The man [standing behind me] told me so."[19] Alden was arrested but was allowed to remain at home under house arrest.

Philip English, a Porter family in-law, also faced the magistrates. Puritan leaders considered the wealthy shipowner a real threat. He had wanted to build an Anglican church in Salem. English escaped prison, but

SOURCE DOCUMENT

THOSE WENCHES BEING PRESENT, WHO PLAID THEIR JUGGLING TRICKS, FALLING DOWN, AND STARING IN PEOPLES FACES, THE MAGISTRATES DEMANDED OF THEM SEVERAL TIMES, WHO IT WAS OF ALL THE PEOPLE IN THE ROOM THAT HURT THEM? ONE OF THESE ACCUSERS POINTED SEVERAL TIMES AT ONE CAPTAIN HILL, THERE PRESENT, BUT SPAKE NOTHING; THE SAME ACCUSER HAD A MAN STANDING AT HER BACK TO HOLD HER UP; HE STOOPED DOWN TO HEAR EAR, THEN SHE CRIED OUT, ALDIN, ALDIN AFFLICTED HER; ONE OF THE MAGISTRATES ASKED HER IF SHE HAD EVER SEEN ALDIN, SHE ANSWERED NO, HE ASKED HER HOW SHE KNEW IT WAS ALDIN? SHE SAID, THE MAN TOLD HER SO. . . .[20]

One afflicted girl claimed that prominent businessman John Alden bewitched her, even though she had never seen him before.

Sheriff George Corwin confiscated most of his property. Daniel Andrew, a wealthy shipper and another in-law of the Porters, also fled the area and went into hiding. Judges made no attempt to round up these influential men.

Many of the accused, such as English and Andrew, had ties to the Porter family. Others, such as Francis Nurse's wife, Rebecca, were related to people who had offended the Putnams or their friends.

Some people, however, were too powerful to touch. Israel and Joseph Porter escaped charges. So did Joseph Putnam, perhaps for a different reason. He had let his brothers know he kept a loaded gun at his side, and he would use it on anyone who tried to arrest him.

"A King in Satan's Kingdom"

Danger greeted each day for the villagers of Wells, Maine, who lived in constant fear of attacks by Indians and their French allies. Many times the village's minister, George Burroughs, had requested troops from the government in Boston. No help had arrived.

Thus the marshals who arrived on May 2, 1692, might have appeared as a godsend. Now, perhaps, the village could live in security. But if the villagers believed the mounted men were there to help them, they were mistaken. The marshal went straight to Burroughs's house and arrested the former Salem Village minister.

When he heard the charges against him, Burroughs could not believe them. How could Ann Putnam, Jr., call him a sorcerer? She had been only two years old when he had left Salem Village. Burroughs found that he had been accused of being the chief wizard of Massachusetts. Cotton Mather would later describe Burroughs as "one who had the promise for being a *King in Satan's kingdom.*"[21]

Whatever the charges, Burroughs knew John Hathorne would not give him a fair examination. The two men had despised each other for years. Shortly after Hathorne's brother William had died, Burroughs married William's widow, Sarah, against Hathorne's wishes. Burroughs and Sarah went to Maine, where she died. Burroughs then remarried. John Hathorne at least partly blamed Burroughs for his sister-in-law's death.

Salem Village girls brought fantastic accusations against their former minister. Abigail Hobbs was released from prison so that she could testify. She claimed she saw the devil in the woods of Maine, near where her former master Burroughs lived. Mercy Lewis testified that Burroughs "carried me to an exceeding high mountain and showed me all the Kingdoms of the Earth and told me that he would give them all to me if I would write in his book, and if I would not he would throw me down and break my neck."[22] George Burroughs, the onetime reverend of the village, now joined the other accused persons in confinement.

"I Found This Province Miserably Harassed"

Increase Mather looked ashore as the *Nonesuch* approached Salem's harbor on May 14. He was not expecting a friendly reception. Massachusetts' most notable minister was bringing home bad news. The colony's charter, for which he had argued in England, was no more. Instead, Massachusetts was now a royal colony.

For Puritan church leaders, the change was a disaster. The new charter gave the vote to all Christian men except Catholics. This meant that the Puritan elite could no longer be assured of controlling the government. Furthermore, Massachusetts lost the right to elect its own governor. The English king now made that decision.

It was not an ideal government for the Puritans, but it was the best Increase Mather could negotiate. At least he had been allowed to choose the colony's officials. Standing next to him was Massachusetts' new governor.

William Phips was no stranger to the colony. He grew up in New England, then married a financially secure woman. Phips built a ship, sailed it to the Bahamas, and found a Spanish galleon's treasure worth three hundred thousand pounds. The English Crown knighted him for his work. His reputation rose further in early 1690. Phips led an expedition that defeated the French in Nova Scotia.

A few months later, however, he led an expedition against Quebec. Everything went wrong. Disease, bad weather, and disagreements among commanders led to disaster. Phips lost nearly a thousand men. The

Colonial Governor William Phips tried to ignore the witch
scandal at first. Later, he freed eight persons who had been
accused of witchcraft.

unsuccessful invasion cost more than fifty thousand pounds. Nonetheless, England's King William trusted Phips's military skills. He wanted someone who could lead battles against the French and their Indian allies. He accepted Increase Mather's choice of William Phips for governor.

The selection of Phips pleased at least one Massachusetts resident. Cotton Mather wrote in his diary, "The time for favor was now come! . . . The Governor of the Province is not my enemy, but one whom I baptized . . . and one of my dearest friends."[23]

Phips expected physical problems in New England, but not supernatural ones. He commented, "I found this province miserably harassed with a most horrible witchcraft or possession of devils. . . . Some scores of poor people were taken with preternatural torments, some scalded with brimstone."[24] More than one hundred fifty people sat in Salem or Boston prisons, accused of being witches. Since the old colonial charter had been dissolved, Massachusetts had had no legal government.

Now, however, the Massachusetts Bay Colony had an official government. Trials could begin. Phips himself had no interest in presiding over the witchcraft trials. He decided to set up a special court to handle the task.

The Court of Oyer and Terminer (from French words meaning "to hear" and "to determine") would handle the witchcraft trials. Phips appointed its members: civic leader Nathaniel Saltonstall, businessmen John Richards and Peter Sergeant, militia general Wait Still Winthrop, author Samuel Sewall, and Bartholomew Gedney (the only Salem Town resident on the court). None had any legal training. Lieutenant Governor William Stoughton, who strongly believed in spectral evidence, was chosen to lead the court. Having made arrangements so that justice could be performed, Phips left to fight against the French and Indians in Maine.

For some, the establishment of a court came too late. Sarah Good had given birth to a child shortly after she entered prison. The infant died a few weeks later. Sarah Osborne, the ailing woman accused by Tituba, also died in custody.

Bridget Bishop

The court wasted no time in trying its first case. Although many people believed in spectral evidence, others had doubts. Cotton Mather wrote court member John Richards, warning him against relying solely on victims' visions. But the case against Bridget Bishop appeared strong, even without evidence that depended upon the deeds of spirits.

Bishop already had a reputation for ill behavior. Years before, she was brought to court for using foul language against her husband. She had called him an old rogue and an old devil on the Sabbath. Her husband had reportedly returned the insults. She and her husband were forced to stand back-to-back for an hour in the public plaza, both gagged, with papers on their foreheads detailing their crime.[25]

Her husband had died several years earlier, but Bridget Bishop's reputation had not improved. For years, she was suspected of practicing the black arts of witchcraft. That reputation was not helped on her way to the courthouse. She glanced at the meetinghouse, and a board fell off its wall. At the trial, two workmen seemingly confirmed the witchcraft suspicion. Both testified that while repairing her home, they found several headless dolls buried in her wall. It was believed that witches used such puppets to cast spells against their enemies.

The puppet evidence helped seal Bridget Bishop's fate. The court found her guilty on June 3. A week later, she was hanged on Gallows Hill. Bridget Bishop became the first person executed for witchcraft in Salem Village. She would not be the last.

7

"DELIVER US FROM EVIL"

Bridget Bishop's death divided uneasy Salem Village even further. Some observers felt the jury's verdict was unjust, and Bishop certainly did not deserve to die. One of these dissidents was court member Nathaniel Saltonstall. He quit the court shortly after the Bishop verdict. He was replaced by Jonathan Corwin.

The examinations, jailings, and trials were taking a toll on Salem Village. Jailings meant that livestock, crops, and property might go untended. Prisoners had to pay their own expenses while confined. That meant that friends or family members often had to sell property to pay these bills. People often had to travel long distances to visit their loved ones.

Nevertheless, most of the village was caught up in the witch scare. Villagers still accepted spectral evidence. They believed that a person's shape or spirit could harm others, even though that person might be many miles away. Some residents tried to persuade accused relatives to confess their sins, whether they were guilty or not. The jailings and trials continued.

The Return of Several Ministers

Saltonstall was not the only prominent person who was troubled by the Bishop hanging. Governor Phips sought the advice of several ministers about what he should do. Twelve ministers, led by Cotton Mather, issued a report that would be crucial to the witch trials.

The Return of Several Ministers Consulted by His Excellency and the Honorable Consul upon the Present Witchcrafts in Salem Village appeared in mid-June. For the most part, it urged caution in the trials. "'Tis necessary that all proceedings thereabout be managed with an exceeding tenderness toward those that may be complained of," the report commented, "especially if they have been persons of an unblemished reputation."[1]

Spectral evidence had to be handled with care, Cotton Mather warned. "Do not lay more stress upon pure specter testimony than it will bear," he advised.[2] Mather suggested using other methods: confessions, occult threats made by suspects, puppets found on the property of the accused, or the presence of witch marks on the body of the accused.

Cotton Mather was stuck in a dilemma. On the one hand, he disapproved of trying people only on spectral evidence. However, he also respected the judges. Many of them were his personal friends. He did not want *The Return of Several Ministers* to appear critical of them.

Therefore, Cotton Mather added a final paragraph to the report. It is not certain whether the other ministers approved his conclusion. It read: "Nevertheless,

Cotton Mather led the twelve ministers who published The
Return of Several Ministers *about the witchcraft trials.*

We cannot but humbly Recommend unto the Government, the speedy and vigorous Prosecution of such as have rendered themselves obnoxious."[3]

The last paragraph changed the whole tone of the report. Before it, *The Return of Several Ministers* provided sound advice to the judges on how to proceed with the trials. Had the judges followed the advice against relying solely on spectral evidence, the trials might have ended immediately. The last sentence, however, appeared to give them license to do whatever they wanted. The judges used that license.

"God Will Give You Blood to Drink!"

Trials began anew on June 28. Neighbors had long harbored suspicions that Susannah Martin was a witch. One claimed that she caused a neighbor's cattle to swim to a nearby island. According to another, she came to visit with her clothes completely dry, even though she had traveled along a watery path. The neighbor perhaps could not fathom that Martin took care not to get her clothing wet.

Cotton Mather later described Susannah Martin as "one of the most impudent, scurrilous, wicked creatures of this world."[4] Yet she claimed she led a virtuous life. She used biblical arguments to refute the charges against her. Nonetheless, the judges found her guilty of witchcraft.

The trials did not proceed without defense of the accused. Even unpopular Sarah Good found someone to speak for her. One of the afflicted girls accused

Good of attacking her with a knife. The girl produced the fragment of a knife.

A spectator saw the knife. He claimed that it had broken off the day before in the girl's presence. The young man then produced the other part of the knife. It fit the fragment perfectly. The accuser did not deny her story. To the judges, truth was less important than conviction. The girl was obviously a liar, yet they allowed her to continue testifying. Sarah Good's protests of innocence did her no good. She, too, was sentenced to death.

Rebecca Nurse, a living example of all that was good in Puritanism, was tried next. When fellow accused witch Deliverance Hobbs was brought to testify against her, Nurse asked why Hobbs was allowed to speak. Nurse said, "She is one of us."[5] She claimed later that she meant Hobbs was a fellow suspect and thus not allowed to testify. Judges took her statement to mean that Hobbs was a fellow witch and convicted Rebecca Nurse.

Nurse's loyal family members refused to take the verdict quietly. They went to Boston and pled their case to Governor Phips. They pointed out the petition in her behalf, her trial (in which she had been found not guilty before the verdict was changed), and an appeal from Rebecca Nurse herself.

The governor, at first, agreed and signed a reprieve for Rebecca Nurse. Then her opponents got his ear. Phips took back the reprieve. Then, he left for the relative tranquillity of battle-infested Maine.

Shortly after the trial, Samuel Parris commented in his diary that Rebecca Nurse's relatives were not attending his church services. Why would they forsake the church at a time when they needed its solace most? Perhaps he wrote this as a self-serving comment for anyone who would read the diary in the future. Or perhaps he could not understand that family members might detest a man who they felt contributed to their relative's death.

In early July, Rebecca Nurse received another terrible blow. Her church in Salem Town voted to excommunicate her. The elderly woman, who had given her life to serving God, might have taken removal from her church as a fate worse than death.

On July 19, Rebecca Nurse, Sarah Good, Susannah Martin, and two others rode to Gallows Hill. Rebecca Nurse took her fate with Christian resignation. She prayed for God to forgive those who had wronged her.

Sarah Good did not go so quietly. Nicholas Noyes, a heavyset man who was a rabid witch hunter, spoke to Good. He told her that she was a witch, and she could save her immortal soul by confessing to witchcraft.

"You're a liar! I am no more a witch than you are a wizard!" she hissed at him. "If you take away my life, God will give you blood to drink!"[6]

Then the logical voice of Susannah Martin, the pious voice of Rebecca Nurse, and the scathing voice of Sarah Good were silenced forever.

Neighbors, Confessors, and Questioners

Joseph Ballard of nearby Andover worried about his ailing wife. He could not identify a physical cause. Ballard sent for some of Salem Village's afflicted girls to find out if witchcraft might be involved. The girls arrived and immediately had fits. To Andover residents, this meant witches must be residing in their town.

Witchcraft hysteria spread beyond Salem in the early summer of 1692. Residents of Malden, Lynn, Beverly, and other towns began eyeing their neighbors suspiciously. Andover, particularly, suffered a witchcraft crisis. Fifty people in Andover were accused.

In Andover, however, suspected witches fought back. An accused Boston merchant filed a one-thousand-pound lawsuit against the girls who cried out on him. The accusers backed off, and the Andover hysteria eventually died down.

The hysteria continued, however, in Salem Village. About fifty people confessed to some form of witchcraft. Many gave wild, unbelievable stories that nevertheless, were accepted without question. Some did so in order to save themselves. It became apparent that those who declared their innocence would be convicted and executed, while those who confessed would be spared. A few had their own reasons for confessing. A woman named Mary Toothaker said she made a pact with the devil to save herself from Indian attacks.

If some confessed, others questioned the procedure of the trials, as well as the confessions. Robert Pike, a Salem magistrate, claimed that demons were tormenting the afflicted girls. Accepting testimony from them would be like accepting testimony from the devil. He also doubted the word of the confessors. If the devil possessed them, how could they be relied on to tell the truth?

John Willard protested in his own way. Willard, a constable, had the job of bringing in accused witches. He quit because he could not stand arresting friends and neighbors who he believed were innocent.

Willard's action enraged the afflicted girls. By now, they had become a major force in the village. They unleashed their wrath on anyone who dared question their actions. The girls cried out on John Willard, and he was arrested.

The girls cried out, directly or indirectly, on many foes. Even ministers were not immune. Reverend John Higginson spoke out against the witchcraft proceedings. The afflicted girls accused his daughter. Samuel Willard, a liberal minister from Boston, helped opponents of the witchcraft proceedings. His nephew, John Proctor, was arrested. George Burroughs ministered to all religions without favoritism. To fanatical Puritans, he was the most dangerous of all.

"Thy Kingdom Come, Thy Will Be Done"

John Proctor, from his Boston prison, heard about the July executions. He would feel the hangman's noose around his neck if he did not take action. On July 23, he sent a petition to five Boston ministers on behalf of himself and other prisoners. He claimed they could not receive a fair trial under the present judges. Proctor urged the ministers to arrange for a different trial site or at least different judges.

Proctor also claimed that prisoners were being tortured to extract confessions. He complained about "Popish cruelties."[7] To strongly Protestant Puritans, comparison to the Catholic pope was a major insult. The clergy, however, declined to act on Proctor's plea.

John Proctor and several others faced trial in August. George Jacobs's granddaughter spoke out against her grandfather and George Burroughs. She tried to retract the charges, but judges refused to allow the retraction. She later apologized to her grandfather and Burroughs. Both accepted the apology.

George Jacobs became indignant when people accused him of being a witch. "You tax me for a wizard,"

SOURCE DOCUMENT

THEY TOLD ME IF I WOULD NOT CONFESS, I SHOULD BE PUT DOWN INTO THE DUNGEON AND WOULD BE HANGED, BUT IF I WOULD CONFESS I SHOULD HAVE MY LIFE; THE WHICH DID SO AFFRIGHT ME, WITH MY OWN VILE WICKED HEART TO SAVE MY LIFE MADE ME MAKE THE CONFESSION I DID, WHICH CONFESSION, MAY IT PLEASE THE HONOURED COURT, IS ALTOGETHER FALSE AND UNTRUE.[8]

Margaret Jacobs tried to retract the charges accusing her grandfather and George Burroughs of witchcraft. The court, however, refused to accept her recantation.

he exclaimed, "you might as well tax me for a buzzard."[9] A judge then asked Jacobs to recite the Lord's Prayer. Many people believed that a witch or wizard could not recite the prayer perfectly. Jacobs made a mistake. His fate was sealed.

Martha Carrier also came to trial. Accused Andover witches claimed that she and George Burroughs were the earthly leaders of the devil's conspiracy to take over the world. Her sons, after being tortured, spoke out against her. Cotton Mather described Carrier as "this rampant hag" who "the devil had promised . . . should be queen of hell."[10]

George Burroughs came to trial with little hope of acquittal. Other accused persons might have offended specific accusers. Burroughs attacked the whole concept of witchcraft. He claimed "there neither are nor ever were witches that having made a compact with the devil can send a devil to torment other people at a distance."[11] Such a statement conflicted with a basic belief of the Puritan ministers. George Burroughs was too dangerous to be allowed to live.

Burroughs's religious views might have been the real reason he was brought to trial. His accusers, however, found other reasons. They attacked him because of his amazing strength, noting that he could lift an entire molasses barrel by himself. They also claimed, completely without evidence, that he was responsible for the deaths of his first two wives.

Increase Mather, Massachusetts' most influential clergyman, had avoided the earlier trials. It is unclear what influenced him to attend the Burroughs hearing. However, he later claimed that if he were a juror, he could not have acquitted Burroughs. The jurors agreed with Increase Mather's opinion.

Five persons—John Proctor, George Burroughs, Martha Carrier, George Jacobs, and John Willard— were sentenced to be hanged on August 19. A sixth, Elizabeth Proctor, escaped the August hanging. Proctor was pregnant, and the Puritans felt an unborn child should not be sacrificed because of the mother's sins. Proctor would be allowed to give birth to her child. *Then* she would be hanged.

Hundreds of people gathered at Gallows Hill to witness the August hangings. Some might have shown up to applaud the death of those they felt were devils. Others came out of curiosity. Many, however, were friends of the accused witches. The atmosphere was tense before the hangings began.

George Burroughs did nothing to ease the tension. His executioners allowed him to speak. Burroughs responded with an impassioned, eloquent plea for his life and the lives of the others. Observer Robert Calef noted, "Mr. Burroughs . . . made a speech . . . with such solemn and serious expressions as were to the admiration of all present. His prayer . . . was so well worded, and uttered with such composedness and such . . . fervency of spirit as . . . drew tears from many."[12]

Judge Samuel Sewall offered a different view. He wrote, "Mr. Burroughs by his speech, prayer, protestation of innocence, did much move unthinking persons,

Samuel Sewall, one of the judges of the Court of Oyer and Terminer, was the only judge who later openly regretted his role in the trials.

which occasions their speaking hardly concerning his being executed."[13]

Burroughs ended his statement by reciting the Lord's Prayer. The crowd, which had been agitated, hushed when the minister spoke. "Our Father, who art in heaven . . . thy kingdom come, thy will be done . . . lead us not into temptation, but deliver us from evil. . . ." He recited the prayer perfectly.

Now it was Cotton Mather, not Burroughs, who was afraid. Burroughs, by reciting the prayer, had shown that he was not a witch. The crowd, many of whom were already skeptical, appeared ready to revolt against the hangings. Such a revolt would bring all the witch trials to question. And if the trials were questioned, so would be the government that had permitted the trials. If a Puritan-based government were questioned, so might be Puritan ministers, including Cotton Mather himself. For Cotton Mather's own sake, as well as that of his fellow ministers, George Burroughs would have to hang.

Cotton Mather, riding on horseback, went through the crowd. He tried to calm them by proving that Burroughs was a witch. He reminded everyone that George Burroughs had never been ordained as a minister. With the crowds calmed somewhat, the hangings proceeded.

The accused witches did not receive a decent burial. All of their bodies were thrown into a makeshift common grave. Burroughs had worn his finest suit to the hanging. Thieves stole the suit and replaced it with inferior clothing.

"More Weight! More Weight!"

The reaction to the hangings left Salem Village leaders uneasy. September's events would not make further trials easier.

Mary Bradbury was one of those who went to trial in early September. The ailing woman practiced healing, sometimes with greater success than local doctors. One accuser charged that she appeared in the shape of a blue boar. Judges would not accept a statement in her behalf by her minister or a petition signed by 115 friends and neighbors. However, they were willing to accept a preposterous boar story. After her conviction, friends helped her escape. Salem authorities did not make a major effort to find her.

Others lacked Bradbury's friends and influence. Martha Corey, Margaret Scott, Mary Easty, Alice Parker, Ann Pudeator, Wilmot Redd, Samuel Wardwell, and Mary Parker—all were tried, convicted, and sentenced to be executed on September 22.

One victim did not live to see the hangings. Feisty Giles Corey, Martha's husband, went before the magistrates. He refused to say whether or not he was guilty of witchcraft. Giles Corey had a reason for his silence. He knew that if he pleaded innocent, he would be found guilty and hanged. If he confessed to witchcraft, he could live, but the government would take away his property. The eighty-year-old Corey realized he would not have long to live anyway. He had signed over his property to sons-in-law who had stood by him and his wife. Corey might have kept silent to assure that the sons-in-law could inherit the property.

Law officers, however, tried to extract a confession from him. They tied his hands and feet, then placed heavy stones on his body. After this torture, they figured, he would testify. According to legend, Corey would not yield. Instead, he shouted to his tormentors, "More weight! More weight!"[14] After two days of being pressed by stones, Giles Corey died. If Salem authorities thought they had scored a victory with his death, they were mistaken. Giles Corey became a folk hero whose admirers wrote a ballad about him.

"No More Innocent Blood Be Shed"

Word of Corey's death must have reached Mary Easty in her jail cell. Her sister, Rebecca Nurse, had already been hanged. Another sister, Sarah Cloyce, was awaiting trial. As for Easty, she had put up a good legal battle. She had requested that favorable testimony on her behalf be included. She also had requested that spectral testimony not be allowed unless there was also other evidence. These pleas went nowhere. Easty knew she would hang the following day.

Mary Easty wrote a letter to the judges and clergymen. "I petition your honors not for my life, for I know I must die, and my appointed time is set," she stated, but asked, "if it be possible, that no more innocent blood be shed."[15]

On the way from the jail to Gallows Hill, a cart carrying some of the prisoners got a wheel stuck in a rut. An afflicted girl cried that the devil was at work, trying to prevent his followers from being executed.

The stuck cart prevented nothing. Eight more people perished in the hangman's noose on September 22. Some took these executions as a sign that justice was being served. The fanatical Nicholas Noyes commented, "What a sad thing it is to see eight firebrands of Hell hanging there."[16]

Others with a different outlook wondered if the madness would ever end.

Colonial Governor Phips returned from Maine on September 29. He was disgusted with what he encountered. Phips had created the Court of Oyer and Terminer for speedy trials. That way, he had hoped, the prisons could be emptied.

Instead, he found conditions worse than when he left. There were still about one hundred

8

"I PUT AN END TO THE COURT"

fifty people in Salem's prison. More than a hundred others were awaiting trial. Some of the prisoners were younger than ten years old.

Accusations by "Scandalous Persons"

Phips had hoped others would solve the witchcraft crisis. Now he saw he would have to take action. First of all, Lieutenant Governor Stoughton had proven incompetent to handle the problem. More important, witchcraft accusations were now facing some of the colony's most important families.

Throughout the summer, the afflicted girls acted with impunity. They accused anyone they pleased, with little fear of retaliation. But as summer turned to fall, they set their charges at a more influential group of people.

Nathaniel Saltonstall, the judge who had resigned from the court, was one of those accused. So were two sons of respected former governor Simon Bradstreet. So was the secretary of Connecticut.

John Hale's defense of the witchcraft trials was as loud as anybody's. At least, it was before a Wenham girl named Mary Herrick cried out on his wife, Sarah. Sarah Hale's specter, said Mary, was pricking and attacking her. Suddenly, the Beverly minister saw the light. When other people were in danger, Hale said nothing. But now that *his* wife was among the accused, he saw the injustice of spectral evidence. Hale said it must have been the devil in disguise who had attacked Mary Herrick.

Margaret Thatcher was one of the wealthiest women in Massachusetts. She was also the mother-in-law of Jonathan Corwin. She was cried out on but never arrested.

Boston minister Samuel Willard was highly regarded by fellow ministers and his congregation. That good reputation was not enough to keep him above suspicion. He published anonymously a document titled *Dialogue Between S[alem] and B[oston]*. In it, he claimed the accusing girls were "scandalous persons, liars, and loose in their conversation."[1]

While Phips was fighting in the northern wilderness, his wife acted at home. With or without her husband's permission, she signed a warrant for the release of someone she knew.

"Cases of Conscience"

Phips still did not know what to do. He wrote a letter to the British government, asking for advice. He hinted "that the Devill had taken upon him the name and shape of several persons who were doubtless innocent."[2] Although he criticized the trials in general, he took care not to complain about specific judges. The letter bought him time. Perhaps the crisis would play itself out.

Others acted more quickly and decisively. Thomas Brattle was a Boston merchant, mathematician, and astronomer. He circulated a letter strongly critical of the trials. His October letter, to an unknown "Reverend Sir," claimed that many magistrates and leading citizens opposed them. Brattle wrote, "Excepting Mr. Hale, Mr. Noyes, and Mr. Parris, the Reverend Elders almost throughout the country are very much dissatisfied."[3] He reserved special criticism for Chief Judge Stoughton, charging that he was "very zealous in these proceedings. Wisdom and counsel are withheld from his honor as to this matter."[4]

Another document circulated at the same time proved even more powerful. Up until now, Increase Mather had not said much about the witchcraft trials. Now his opinion would be known. *Cases of Conscience Concerning Evil Spirits Personating Men, Witchcrafts, infallible Proofs of Guilt in such as are accused with that*

Crime was not published until 1693. Nonetheless, the tract's beliefs were made known to Massachusetts leaders. Spectral evidence should not be used unless some other kind of evidence—confessions, observations of harmful deeds by physical bodies, inability to say prayers, or supernatural attributes of the accused—was also present. By itself, spectral evidence could be deceptive. "Satan seems to be what he is not, and makes others seem to be what they are not," Increase Mather warned.[5]

Cases of Conscience declared, "It is better that ten suspected witches should escape than that one innocent person be condemned."[6] Nonetheless, Increase Mather praised the judges as "wise and good men" who acted "with all Fidelity according to their Light."[7] Every major Boston minister signed the document except one: Increase's son, Cotton Mather.

With powerful ministers opposing spectral evidence, Phips felt he could act. He sent a letter to leading New York clergy, seeking their opinion. He did not wait for a response before his next major action.

The Court of Oyer and Terminer had been in recess since September. On October 12, he forbade any further imprisonments or trials for witchcraft. Near the end of October, someone asked him when the court would resume its sessions. Phips declared that the court "must fall."[8] His declaration ended the Court of Oyer and Terminer.

Increase Mather wrote, "It is better that ten suspected witches should escape than that one innocent person be condemned." His influential writing helped put an end to the witchcraft trials.

"That Reviled Book"

Cotton Mather did not sit back and watch the events without criticism. Soon after other ministers released *Cases of Conscience*, Cotton Mather revealed his own book. *Wonders of the Invisible World* was a hodgepodge of sermons, letters, and commentaries on witchcraft. It also included transcripts of five trials, apparently given to Mather by Chief Judge Stoughton.

The book was an attempt to justify the trials. After all, the court was leading a necessary fight against an "Army of Devils."[9] It might also have been an attempt to justify the actions of his friends on the courts.

Mather did not include accounts of the trials of obviously innocent people like Rebecca Nurse or John Proctor. Instead, he described the trials where evidence other than spectral evidence was included. George Burroughs had boasted of occult powers and had shown amazing strength. Bridget Bishop had puppets in her home. Susannah Martin and Martha Carrier did not have good reputations even before the trials.

As an attempt to persuade the population, *Wonders* was a failure. Part of the problem lay in the book's tone. Cotton Mather claimed that the book "is not written with an evil spirit."[10] But merchant and author Robert Calef claimed that Mather "wrote more like an advocate than an historian."[11]

Other people also failed to go along with Cotton Mather's ideas. Massachusetts residents had become increasingly appalled by the violence. Nineteen people had been hanged, one pressed to death, and others

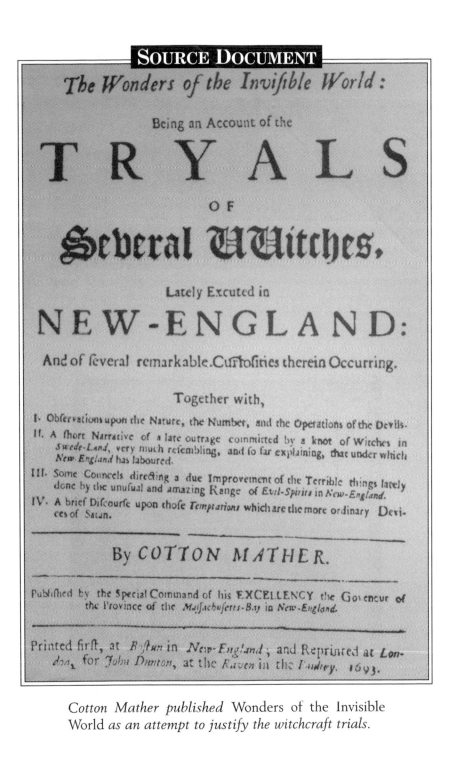

The Wonders of the Invisible World:

Being an Account of the

T R Y A L S

O F

Several Witches,

Lately Excuted in

NEW-ENGLAND:

And of several remarkable Curiosities therein Occurring.

Together with,

I. Observations upon the Nature, the Number, and the Operations of the Devils.

II. A short Narrative of a late outrage committed by a knot of Witches in Swede-Land, very much resembling, and so far explaining, that under which New-England has laboured.

III. Some Councels directing a due Improvement of the Terrible things lately done by the unusual and amazing Range of Evil-Spirits in New-England.

IV. A brief Discourse upon those Temptations which are the more ordinary Devices of Satan.

By COTTON MATHER.

Published by the Special Command of his EXCELLENCY the Governeur of the Province of the Massachusetts-Bay in New-England.

Printed first, at Boston in New-England; and Reprinted at London, for John Dunton, at the Raven in the Poultrey. 1693.

Cotton Mather published Wonders of the Invisible World *as an attempt to justify the witchcraft trials.*

perished in prison. Too many people were being accused. Most people knew among the accused at least one friend or relative whom they felt could not possibly be guilty.

Mather realized that *Wonders of the Invisible World* was a failure. Later in life, he referred to it in his diary as "that reviled book."[12]

Cotton Mather was not the only one whose reputation suffered. The afflicted girls only a few months earlier were perhaps the most powerful people in Salem Village. But in November, they encountered an old woman on the road. Immediately they began screeching and screaming. The other travelers on the road ignored them.

An End to the Court

Even if no new accused persons were to be tried, a problem persisted. What should be done with the people in prison or awaiting trial? Phips created a new court of judicature (justice). He appointed its judges, many of whom had served on the Oyer and Terminer court. Stoughton again was chief justice.

But this new court had one major difference from the old one. Spectral evidence would not be permitted in the trials. For most suspects, this left little evidence against them. They were released.

Trials began for the remaining accused witches in January 1693. Only three of more than fifty accused witches were convicted. Calef called the three convicted people "the most senseless and ignorant creatures that can be found."[13] Stoughton signed death warrants on them and five other persons.

Phips refused to accept these decisions. He signed reprieves for all eight people.

An irate Stoughton, when he heard of the reprieves, left the bench. "We were in a way to have cleared the land of these [witches]," Stoughton cried. "The Lord be merciful to the country."[14]

The governor, in turn, blamed Stoughton for the witchcraft trials scandal: "The Deputy Governor . . . persisted . . . to the great dissatisfaction and disturbance of the people, until I put an end to the court and stopped the proceedings."[15]

Phips finally got answers to his requests for advice. The New York ministers he polled opposed spectral evidence in trials. Such evidence should not be used to condemn people who lived otherwise righteous lives. The response of the long-awaited letter from London was vague. By mid-April, the responses meant little. There were no new trials. In May, Phips issued a general reprieve. Everyone was freed.

Lydia Dustin would not enjoy this reprieve. Many prisoners had been released as soon as someone paid their way out. Many of those still imprisoned were impoverished. They had no family or friends to help them. Dustin was one of those unlucky souls. She, her daughter, and her granddaughter languished in a cell. The eighty-year-old woman was acquitted in early 1693. Still, there was no one to pay her prison bills. Dustin died in prison on March 10.

9

"SURVIVING SUFFERERS"

Life went on at Salem Village in 1693 and afterward. But it was not the same life the residents had known before. Scars—both mental and physical—remained in the village for years.

"So Harshly Used and Terrifyed"

For the most part, the afflicted girls led the same lives they had led before the witchcraft crisis—quiet lives, destined for anonymity. Some reportedly became delinquents. Betty Parris married and had children. The rest of Abigail Williams's life story is unknown.

Reverend Samuel Parris refused to retrieve Tituba from prison. She was sold to a Virginia man who paid for her jail expenses. No further record exists of John Indian. He might have been sold with Tituba.

Elizabeth Proctor gave birth to the baby who had saved her from the gallows. She, along with many others, fought for the property that had been taken from her.

Sheriff George Corwin, who had seized the property of many accused witches, was forced out of office. Philip English was one person who claimed his property was taken illegally. He charged that he was owed fifteen hundred pounds. When Corwin died in 1697, English threatened to seize Corwin's corpse until the debt was repaid. Corwin's estate finally gave him little more than sixty pounds, a fraction of what he had requested.

Mary Toothaker claimed that in May 1692 she had made a pact with the devil, to protect herself and her family from Indians. Three years later, Indians killed Mary and took her twelve-year-old daughter.

Dorcas Good had been described as healthy and good-looking when she was first brought to prison. Her months as a captive had profoundly disturbed her. Dorcas's father, William Good, commented in 1710 that "being chained in the dungeon [she] was so hardly [harshly] used and terrifyed that she hath ever since been very changeable having little or no reason to govern herself."[1]

"We Do Heartily Ask Forgiveness"

Samuel Sewall handed a note to a minister in 1697 and stood silently while the minister read his confession to the congregation. Entries in Sewall's diary suggested that he sincerely regretted his role as a member of the court during the trials.

Reverend John Hale of Beverly still believed people were practicing witchcraft. However, he was troubled by the witchcraft trials. In 1697, Hale wrote *A Modest Enquiry into the Nature of Witchcraft*. The book was published in 1702, after his death. In it, Hale declared,

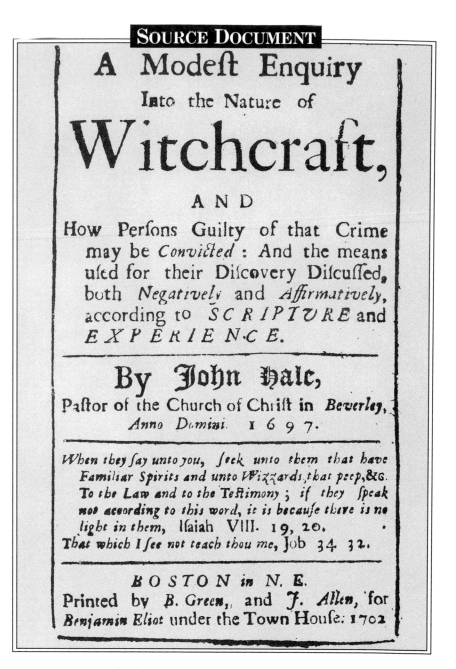

A Modest Enquiry

Into the Nature of

Witchcraft,

AND

How Persons Guilty of that Crime may be *Convicted* : And the means used for their Discovery Discussed, both *Negatively* and *Affirmatively*, according to *SCRIPTURE* and *EXPERIENCE.*

By 𝔍𝔬𝔥𝔫 𝔥𝔞𝔩𝔢,

Pastor of the Church of Christ in *Beverley,* *Anno Domini.* 1 6 9 7.

When they say unto you, seek unto them that have Familiar Spirits and unto Wizzards, that peep, &c. To the Law and to the Testimony ; if they speak not according to this word, it is because there is no light in them, Isaiah VIII. 19, 20. *That which I see not teach thou me,* Job 34. 32.

BOSTON in N. E.
Printed by B. Green, and J. Allen, for
Benjamin Eliot under the Town House: 1702

Reverend John Hale wrote A Modest Enquiry into the Nature of Witchcraft. *In it, he confessed, "There has been a great deal of innocent blood shed."*

There has been a great deal of innocent blood shed . . . by proceeding upon unsafe principles, in condemning persons for Malefick Witchcraft. . . . We have cause to be humbled for the mistakes and errors . . . in their Proceedings against persons for this crime.[2]

Historian Perry Miller described it as a "sad, troubled, and honest book."[3]

Twelve of the jurors also issued a public apology in 1697. Their declaration of regret declared,

We do signify to all in general, and to the surviving sufferers in special, our deep sense of, and sorrow for, our errors. . . . We do heartily ask forgiveness of you all . . . and do declare, according to our present minds, we would none of us do such things again, on such grounds, for the whole world.[4]

Ann Putnam, Jr., appeared before the church in 1706. Her parents had both died in 1699. After their deaths, she assumed the responsibility of caring for her brothers and sisters.

"I justly fear I have been instrumental with others . . . to bring upon myself and this land the guilt of innocent blood," she confessed. "I did it not for any anger, malice or ill will to any person for I had no such things against one of them, but what I did was ignorantly, being deluded of Satan."[5] Putnam, who never married, died eleven years later.

"More Wonders"

Not everyone publicly or privately regretted their roles in the witchcraft trials. John Hathorne and William

Stoughton never uttered a word of apology. Both continued to be community leaders and lived to old age.

If John Hathorne was not embarrassed by his performance, one of his descendants was. Famed novelist Nathaniel Hawthorne, great-great-grandson of the judge, changed his name because he was ashamed of his ancestor's actions during the witchcraft trials.

Cotton Mather never publicly regretted his actions during the trials. If he did not criticize himself, others were willing to attack him. Robert Calef, a Boston merchant, was a particularly harsh critic. In 1700, Calef wrote *More Wonders of the Invisible World*. This book was a direct attack on Cotton Mather's *Wonders of the Invisible World*. Calef's book examined some of the witchcraft trials Cotton Mather had ignored, such as those of Rebecca Nurse and John Proctor. The book

Famous author Nathaniel Hawthorne changed his last name because he was ashamed of his great-great-grandfather's actions as a judge in the Salem witchcraft trials.

also included interviews with prominent persons tried, including John Alden and Nathaniel and Elizabeth Cary. Mather's book defended the trials because they fought the evils of witchcraft. Calef claimed the trials themselves were evil. He said Cotton Mather "conduced much to the kindling of these flames" that "threatened the destruction of this country."[6]

Increase Mather condemned this attack on his son's book. He publicly burned a copy of *More Wonders of the Invisible World* at Harvard Square. Even so, Cotton Mather became a laughingstock in some parts of Boston society.

Nicholas Noyes died of a hemorrhage twenty-five years after the trials. According to legend, blood poured from his mouth—an eerie fulfillment of Sarah Good's curse.

"His Removal from Thence"

The end of the witchcraft trials did not mean the end of Samuel Parris's woes. If anything, opposition to him, led by the family of Rebecca Nurse, intensified. Battles over his ministry would continue for several years.

Opponents asked him to call other ministers to the village to resolve the disputes. In late 1693, Parris agreed to arrange a conference of ministers. He delayed more than a year in doing so.

Seven ministers and ten elders from Boston-area churches met at Salem Village in the spring of 1695. Increase Mather, still one of the most respected Massachusetts clergymen, served as moderator of the council. The religious leaders suggested that Salem villagers retain their minister, but they gave him a way to make a graceful exit. They commented that if hostilities should force Parris to leave, "his removal from thence will not expose him to any hard character with us."[7]

Despite this less than hearty support, Parris remained in Salem Village two more years. In 1697, he accepted a payment of £79 from the village. In return, he surrendered the parsonage.

Parris went to a ministry in western Massachusetts. Once again, he got into a dispute over salary. He later served as a schoolmaster and merchant. Samuel Parris died in 1720. Among the "possessions" sold after his death was a female slave named Violet. She may have been the daughter of Tituba and John Indian.

Salem Village's next minister was the opposite of Parris in temperament. By now, experienced ministers wanted no part of troubled Salem Village. The villagers had to recruit a younger person. Joseph Green, a recent Harvard seminary graduate, took over the troubled congregation. His pleasant personality soon won over the divided parishioners. He seated Putnams and Nurses, bitter enemies from the witchcraft trials, next to each other on the same bench. This move helped the families deal with their differences.

Restitution

Good feeling was not enough for many Salem Village residents. They wanted apologies for their suffering and that of their families. Many demanded cash settlements. They said property had been taken from them illegally. Philip English claimed he had lost £1,500 to Salem authorities. Others complained of lost cash or property.

English received no repayment from the government during his lifetime. After his death, the colony awarded his heirs £200. Survivors of some of those executed received money in 1711. John and Elizabeth Proctor's family received £150. Giles and Martha Corey's heirs got £21. The Good family was granted £30. That amount was less a payment for the late Sarah Good than an apology for the mental damage done to young Dorcas Good.

Reverend Joseph Green realized that many parishioners wanted to clear their relatives' good names. In 1702, he asked the congregation to revoke the excommunication of Martha Corey. Five years later, the church complied. In 1712, Rebecca Nurse and Giles Corey regained their status as honored members of the church.

In 1711, the government officially overturned the convictions of twenty-two of the thirty-one people found guilty during the trials. The remaining nine were people who did not have families to speak on their behalf. In 1957—265 years after the last of the trials— the state of Massachusetts reversed their convictions.

10

"SWEPT ALONG BY THE FRENZY"

A saintly old woman named Rebecca Nurse. A pipe-smoking beggar named Sarah Good and her newborn child. An outspoken tavern owner named John Proctor. A brash woman named Martha Carrier. An eloquent minister named George Burroughs. A forgiving grandfather named George Jacobs. An eccentric widow named Bridget Bishop. A bedridden woman named Sarah Osborne. A stubborn old man named Giles Corey. A conscience-stricken public servant named John Willard. Common people named Alice Parker, Samuel Wardwell, and Margaret Scott. All of these people might have looked with hope on the year 1692. By the end of the year, all were dead. Either directly—by hanging or in Giles Corey's case, being pressed to death, or indirectly—perishing from horrible conditions in prison, all were victims of the Salem witchcraft hysteria.

History records what happened at the examinations, trials, and executions. But it fails to answer one very important question: Why did this hideous and hysterical event take place?

Witches, Pranksters, and Fungi

In the last three centuries, people have come up with dozens of theories about what caused the witchcraft hysteria. Many have not held up over the years.

Some people at the time saw the trials as God's punishment for an unfaithful colony. Historian Richard Trask noted some later theories:

> pranks of bored adolescents, the influence of . . . power-hungry clergy, local petty jealousies and land grabs . . . spiritualist goings-on, political instability, a . . . holding action against the disintegration of Puritanism, mass clinical hysteria, a clash between agrarian and emerging commercial interests, a continuation of the suppression of certain types of women, and even physical reaction to the ingestion [swallowing] of fungus.[1]

Those theories ignore one possibility—that some of the people accused might have actually been practicing witchcraft. Even if they had not allied themselves with the devil, many people in seventeenth-century New England dabbled in the art of witchcraft. For many years, magical arts had been a part of folk culture, practiced alongside organized religion. A spell cast to gain good fortune or to cure a friend's disease was no evil curse, but it was a spell just the same. The puppets in Bridget Bishop's cellar, for example, might have come from witchcraft attempts.

Charles Upham, a nineteenth-century Salem resident, wrote a book titled *Salem Witchcraft*. In it, he theorized that the afflicted girls might have started by playing pranks, but those pranks had backfired with deadly results. Upham claimed,

> It was perhaps their original design to gratify a love of notoriety or of mischief by creating a sensation and excitement in their neighborhood, or at the worst to wreak their vengeance upon one or two individuals who had offended them. They soon, however, became intoxicated by the terrible success of their imposture, and were swept along by the frenzy they had occasioned.[2]

When asked why she cried out upon a neighbor, one girl responded, "It was for sport. I must have some sport."[3]

One unusual theory claimed the hysteria had a biological origin. Ergotism, a disease contracted through contaminated grain, was once proposed as a possible factor in the Salem outbreak. Ergotism had affected villages in Europe with similar results—mania, psychosis, and delusions. The afflicted girls had complained of symptoms resembling biting, pinching, and choking. These were common ergot symptoms. However, several observers claimed that the afflicted girls in Salem seemed to turn their symptoms on and off at will. They could not have done this if the symptoms came from an organic disease. The ergotism theory was eventually refuted.

Was There a Conspiracy?

Some historians dismiss the Salem mania as mass hysteria, a panic that grabbed most or all of the population of the village. Others claim the trials were part of a plan by one faction in Salem Village to destroy its opposition. They use patterns of accusers and accused to back this theory.

Much of the hysteria was concentrated in a small band of individuals. Most of the accusers lived in the western part of Salem Village. The accused mainly lived in the eastern part, closer to Salem Town. Only a handful of people, mainly young women, claimed to be afflicted. These girls had connections to the powerful Putnam family. Ann Putnam, Jr., was the daughter of Thomas Putnam, who claimed his inheritance was wrongly given to half-brother Joseph Putnam. Mercy Lewis was the Putnams' servant. Betty Parris was the daughter and Abigail Williams the niece of Samuel Parris, who came to his minister's job largely through the backing of the Putnam family. Mary Walcott was the daughter of Jonathan Walcott, related to the Putnams by marriage. Elizabeth Hubbard was the great-niece of the wife of Dr. William Griggs, a Putnam family ally.

The girls claimed afflictions, but their elders signed formal complaints against the accused witches. Once again, the same names appeared on many of the complaints: Thomas Putnam and his brother Edward; their uncles, John Putnam, Sr., and Nathaniel Putnam; Thomas's cousins Jonathan and John Putnam, Jr.; and

Thomas Putnam's brother-in-law, Jonathan Walcott. Innkeeper Nathaniel Ingersoll was Walcott's uncle. Along with two nonrelatives—Reverend Samuel Parris and Dr. William Griggs—he frequently served as a witness.

Thomas Putnam and Samuel Parris particularly were known as harsh masters of their households. Some historians believe they might have fed hints to the girls. The girls, out of willingness or fear, then cried out on Putnam enemies.

A common thread tied together many of the accused. In one way or another, each had offended the Putnam family or its allies. John Putnam, Sr., believed Sarah Osborne had tried to take inheritance money that belonged to two of his nephews. John Proctor ran a tavern that rivaled that of Nathaniel Ingersoll. Proctor's wife, Elizabeth, was a midwife; her work competed with Dr. Griggs's medical practice. George Burroughs had married the sister-in-law of magistrate and Putnam ally Jonathan Hathorne, and she died soon afterward. Rebecca Nurse herself did no known harm to anyone. But her husband, Francis, was part of the council that had voted to cut off Samuel Parris's salary in 1691.

Most of the accused, however, had no such direct connections. Several accused witches were business and merchant leaders of the colony. They represented worldly interference with the austere Puritan lifestyle. Thus, wealthy Boston merchant John Alden, whom the girls knew only by reputation, could be called to Salem Village for an examination.

Few people in Salem Village had a more direct link to witchcraft than Mary Sibley. It was she who told Tituba how to make the forbidden witch cake. Yet Mary Sibley was never hanged, condemned, or even charged. Mary Sibley was a sister-in-law of Jonathan Walcott, and thus part of the Putnam family. She was also a Puritan woman, while Tituba was a West Indian slave. In the early stages of the trials, the issue of ethnicity may have played some role in sparing Sibley.

Yet the real objects of Putnam hatred—the leaders of the Porter family—remained untouched. The object of a Putnam conspiracy might have been to destroy its opposition bit by bit. Israel Porter, Joseph Putnam, and Joseph Porter might have been the final targets. If this was a conspiracy plan, it failed.

Salem and Salem Village Today

Modern Salem has not ignored the witchcraft chapter of the area's history. Tourists and researchers can visit magistrate Jonathan Corwin's house or any of several museums devoted to Salem witchcraft. The witch has become the unofficial town symbol.

In the middle of town, next to an old cemetery, lies the Salem Witch Trials Tercentenary Memorial. It is a small park, surrounded on three sides by a granite wall. Stone benches on the memorial's perimeter bear the names and execution dates of the victims.

Just a few miles away is the town of Danvers. The separate town of Danvers was incorporated from Salem Village and surrounding precincts in 1752. By then, all of the principal persons involved in the witchcraft scare were long dead.

Signs of the witch-trial era remain here as well. The Witchcraft Victims' Memorial on Hobart Street honors the memory of the twenty-five persons who died as a result of the witch-hunt. Chains on the monument symbolize the imprisonment and repression that many people suffered.

Danvers has also saved Rebecca Nurse's homestead. It contains the Nurse family's farmhouse and

A solemn memorial at Danvers, formerly known as Salem Village, honors the innocent persons who died during the witchcraft controversy.

other buildings. The Nurse family cemetery lies at the bottom of a hill. Rebecca Nurse's remains were thrown into a common grave after her hanging. Family members are believed to have dug up her body, then buried it at an unmarked site here. The reinterred remains of another executed person, George Jacobs, are also buried here. A monument on the grounds honors Rebecca Nurse's life.

In a back lot behind a Danvers house lie the remains of Salem Village's parsonage. It had been abandoned in 1784. Excavation began on the site of the house in 1970. The dig yielded thousands of artifacts. Three centuries ago, Samuel and Betty Parris, Abigail Williams, Tituba, and others used these items.

A wooden fence guards a reproduction of the Rebecca Nurse house. Nurse's homestead, in the present-day town of Danvers, has been preserved as a historical site.

A 1970 archaeological project excavated the former residence of Samuel Parris, Betty Parris, and Abigail Williams. The dig yielded clues to everyday life in the late 1600s, but nothing new about the Salem witch controversy.

They included bottles, jugs, and plates—the type of implements that give valuable clues to a household's everyday life.

The excavation, however, did not yield clues to the witchcraft scare. Who or what caused it? Were the Parris family members active participants in a conspiracy, or unwitting accessories to a general calamity? The truth about the cause of the witchcraft hysteria made never be known for certain.

Whatever Samuel Parris's role, he summarized the horror of the witch trials well. He wrote in his diary in March 1692: "The devil hath been raised amongst us, & his Rage vehement & terrible, & when he shall be silenc'd the Lord only knows."[4]

★ TIMELINE ★

1630—Puritan religious refugees establish a colony at Massachusetts Bay.

1653—Oliver Cromwell takes over as Lord High Protector of England.

1660—Parliament reestablishes a monarchy in England; Charles II takes the throne.

1672—James Bayley becomes Salem Village's first minister.

1675—King Philip's War, between Massachusetts settlers and Indians, inflicts heavy casualties on both sides.

1680—George Burroughs becomes Salem Village minister.

1684—Charles II revokes Massachusetts Bay charter.

1685—James II becomes king of England.

1686—Deodat Lawson takes over as Salem Village's third minister.

1688—Glorious Revolution overthrows James II; William and Mary assume English throne.

1689—Puritans overthrow Sir Edmund Andros, English-appointed Massachusetts governor; Samuel Parris becomes Salem Village's fourth minister.

1690—New England's attempted invasion of Quebec fails.

1691—Opponents of Samuel Parris take over town's council, and vote against new pay for the minister's salary.

1692—*January*: Betty Parris has unexplained illness; Dr. William Griggs determines cause must be witchcraft.
February 29: Complaints of witchcraft are made against three local women—Sarah Good, Sarah Osborne, and Parris's slave Tituba.
March: Former minister Deodat Lawson visits Salem Village, sees what he believes are signs of witchcraft; Martha Corey is arrested for witchcraft.
May: Increase Mather and Governor William Phips arrive in Boston with Massachusetts' new charter; Phips establishes Court of Oyer and Terminer.

June: Bridget Bishop is tried, convicted, and executed for witchcraft; Twelve prominent ministers issue *The Return of Several Ministers*; Sarah Good and Rebecca Nurse are convicted of witchcraft.

July 19: Sarah Good, Rebecca Nurse, Susannah Martin, Sarah Wildes, and Elizabeth Howe are hanged; John Proctor, from prison, requests help from Massachusetts' ministers.

August 18: John Proctor, George Burroughs, John Willard, George Jacobs, and Martha Carrier are hanged.

September 22: Martha Corey, Mary Easty, Alice Parker, Ann Pudeator, Margaret Scott, Wilmot Redd, Samuel Wardwell, and Mary Parker are hanged.

October: Increase Mather and other ministers circulate *Cases of Conscience Concerning Evil Spirits Personating Men*, a document often credited with ending the witchcraft trials; Phips terminates Court of Oyer and Terminer.

1693—*January*: Trials begin for remaining accused witches; Most accused witches are freed.

May: Phips issues a reprieve, freeing the remaining accused witches.

1697—Reverend John Hale writes *A Modest Enquiry into the Nature of Witchcraft*, which claims witchcraft judges were good people who made major mistakes; Samuel Parris resigns as Salem Village minister.

1700—Robert Calef publishes *More Wonders of the Invisible World*, which severely criticizes the witchcraft trials.

1706—Ann Putnam, Jr., a ringleader of the accusing girls, apologizes for her role in the trials.

1711—Reparations begin for victims and families of Salem witchcraft trials.

1712—Salem church reinstates Giles Corey and Rebecca Nurse posthumously.

1957—Massachusetts legislature reverses convictions of the remaining accused Salem witches.

★ CHAPTER NOTES ★

Chapter 1. "What Sin Hath God Found in Me?"

1. Deborah Kent, *Salem Massachusetts* (Parsippany, N.J.: Dillon, 1996), p. 26.

2. Paul Boyer and Stephen Nissenbaum, *Salem Possessed: The Social Origins of Witchcraft* (Cambridge, Mass.: Harvard University, 1974), p. 148.

3. Chadwick Hansen, *Witchcraft at Salem* (New York: George Braziller, 1969), p. 127.

4. Marion Starkey, *The Devil in Massachusetts: A Modern Enquiry into the Salem Witch Trials* (Garden City, N.Y.: Anchor, 1969), p. 161.

Chapter 2. "Thou Shalt Not Suffer a Witch to Live"

1. Chadwick Hansen, *Witchcraft at Salem* (New York: George Braziller, 1969), p. 10.

2. Jeffrey B. Russell, *A History of Witchcraft: Sorcerers, Heretics, and Pagans* (New York: Thames and Hudson, 1980), pp. 68–69.

3. Editors of Time-Life Books, *Witches and Witchcraft* (Alexandria, Va.: Time-Life, 1990), p. 64.

4. Ibid., p. 66.

5. Ibid., p. 8.

6. Rossell Hope Robbins, *Encyclopedia of Witchcraft and Demonology*, quoted in Jeffrey B. Russell, *A History of Witchcraft: Sorcerers, heretics, and Pagans* (New York: Thames and Hudson, 1980), p. 82.

7. Editors of Time-Life Books, p. 78.

Chapter 3. "City on a Hill"

1. Paul Boyer and Stephen Nissenbaum, *Salem Possessed: The Social Origins of Witchcraft* (Cambridge, Mass.: Harvard University, 1974), p. 104.

2. Francis Jennings, *The Invasion of America* (New York: W. W. Norton, 1976), p. 180.

3. Michael G. Hall, *The Last American Puritan: The Life of Increase Mather* (Middletown, Conn.: Wesleyan University, 1988), p. 13.

4. Selma R. Williams, *Kings, Commoners, and Colonists: Puritan Politics in Old and New England* (New York: Atheneum, 1974), p. 13.

5. Ibid., p. 86.

6. Carol F. Karlsen, *The Devil in the Shape of a Woman: Witchcraft in Colonial New England* (New York: Vintage, 1989), p. 185.

7. Hall, p. 5.

8. Frances Hill, *A Delusion of Satan: The Full Story of the Salem Witch Trials* (New York: Doubleday, 1995), p. 8.

9. Paul Boyer and Stephen Nissenbaum, eds., *Salem-Village Witchcraft: A Documentary Record of Local Conflict in Colonial New England* (Boston: Northeastern University, 1993), p. 156.

10. Henry W. Lawrence, *The Not-Quite Puritans* (Boston: Little, Brown, 1928), p. 121.

11. Hall, p. 143.

12. Marc Mappen, ed., *Witches and Historians: Interpretations of Salem* (Malibar, Fla.: Krieger, 1980), p. 61.

13. Ibid., p. 62.

14. Hall, p. 191.

15. Elaine G. Breslaw, *Tituba, Reluctant Witch of Salem: Devilish Indians and Puritan Fancies* (New York: New York University, 1996), p. 100.

16. Chadwick Hansen, *Witchcraft at Salem* (New York: George Braziller, 1969), p. xiii.

17. Enders Robinson, *The Devil Discovered: Salem Witchcraft 1692* (New York: Hippocrene, 1991), p. 44.

18. John Putnam Demos, *Entertaining Satan: Witchcraft and the Culture of Early New England* (Oxford, England: Oxford University, 1982), p. 310.

19. Deborah Kent, *Salem Massachusetts* (Parsippany, N.J.: Dillon, 1996), p. 14.

20. Karlsen, p. 28.

21. Kenneth Silverman, *The Life and Times of Cotton Mather* (New York: Harper and Row, 1984), p. 84.

Chapter 4. "Neighbors Against Neighbors"

1. David Freeman Hawke, *Everyday Life in Early America: A Documentary History of the Salem Witchcraft Outbreak of March 1962* (New York: Harper and Row, 1988), p. 161.

2. Richard B. Trask, *The Devil Hath Been Raised: A Documentary History of the Salem Village Outbreak of March 1692* (Danvers, Mass.: Yeoman, 1997), p. xi.

3. Interview with Richard B. Trask, September 26, 1997.

4. Trask, *The Devil Hath Been Raised*, p. xii.

5. Paul Boyer and Stephen Nissenbaum, *Salem Possessed: The Social Origins of Witchcraft* (Cambridge, Mass.: Harvard University, 1974), p. 41.

6. Ibid., p. 54.

7. Paul Boyer and Stephen Nissenbaum, eds., *Salem-Village Witchcraft: A Documentary Record of Local Conflict in Colonial New England* (Boston: Northeastern University, 1993) p. 124.

8. Frances Hill, *A Delusion of Satan: The Full Story of the Salem Witch Trials* (New York: Doubleday, 1995), p. 61.

9. Boyer and Nissenbaum, *Salem Possessed*, p. 161.

Chapter 5. "Suspicion of Witchcraft"

1. Enders Robinson, *The Devil Discovered: Salem Witchcraft 1692* (New York: Hippocrene, 1991), p. 134.

2. Paul Boyer and Stephen Nissenbaum, eds., *Salem-Village Witchcraft: A Documentary Record of Local Conflict in Colonial New England* (Boston: Northeastern University, 1993), p. 97.

3. Robinson, p. 262.

4. Elaine G. Breslaw, *Tituba, Reluctant Witch of Salem: Devilish Indians and Puritan Fancies* (New York: New York University, 1996), p. 107.

5. Chadwick Hansen, *Witchcraft at Salem* (New York: George Braziller, 1969), p. 32.

6. Boyer and Nissenbaum, p. 11.

7. Breslaw, p. 118.

Chapter 6. "These Folks That Are Out of Their Wits"

1. Chadwick Hansen, *Witchcraft at Salem* (New York: George Braziller, 1969), p. 1.

2. Enders Robinson, *The Devil Discovered: Salem Witchcraft 1692* (New York: Hippocrene, 1991), p. 144.

3. Ibid.

4. Hansen, p. 41.

5. Robinson, p. 142.

6. Ibid.

7. Elaine G. Breslaw, *Tituba, Reluctant Witch of Salem: Devilish Indians and Puritan Fancies* (New York: New York University, 1996), p. 136.

8. Francis Hill, *A Delusion of Satan: The Full Story of the Salem Witch Trials* (New York: Doubleday, 1995), p. 81.

9. Marion Starkey, *The Devil in Massachusetts: A Modern Enquiry into the Salem Witch Trials* (Garden City, N.Y.: Anchor, 1969), p. 82.

10. Robinson, p. 152.

11. Starkey, p. 75.

12. Robinson, p. 172.

13. Hansen, p. 63.

14. Ibid., p. 57.

15. Hill, p. 148.

16. Samuel P. Fowler, Esq., *An Account of the Life and Character of Rev. Samuel Parris of Salem Village and His Connections with the Witchcraft Delusion of 1692* (Salem, Mass.: The New England and Virginia Company, 1997), p. 3.

17. Hansen, p. 106.

18. Robinson, p. 330.

19. Starkey, p. 144.

20. Paul Boyer and Stephen Nissenbaum, eds., *Salem-Village Witchcraft: A Documentary Record of Local Conflict in Colonial New England* (Boston: Northeastern University, 1993), p. 120.

21. Robinson, p. 87.

22. Ibid., p. 180.

23. Ibid., p. 32.

24. Hill, p. 154.

25. Boyer and Nissenbaum, p. 156.

Chapter 7. "Deliver Us From Evil"

1. Chadwick Hansen, *Witchcraft at Salem* (New York: George Braziller, 1969), p. 124.

2. Ibid., p. 96.

3. Kenneth Silverman, *The Life and Times of Cotton Mather* (New York: Harper and Row, 1984), p. 100.

4. Enders Robinson, *The Devil Discovered: Salem Witchcraft 1692* (New York: Hippocrene, 1991), p. 211.

5. Marion Starkey, *The Devil in Massachusetts: A Modern Enquiry into the Salem Witch Trials* (Garden City, N.Y.: Anchor, 1969), p. 161.

6. Paul Boyer and Stephen Nissenbaum, *Salem Possessed: The Social Origins of Witchcraft* (Cambridge, Mass.: Harvard University, 1974), pp. 7–8.

7. Starkey, p. 190.

8. G. Lincoln Burr, *Narratives of the Witchcraft Cases 1648–1706*, Quoted in Richard Weisman, *Witchcraft, Magic, and Religion in 17th Century Massachusetts* (Cambridge, Mass.: University of Massachusetts, 1984), p. 157.

9. Starkey, p. 194.

10. Richard Goldstein, ed., *Mine Eyes Have Seen: A First-Person Account of the Events That Shaped America* (New York: Touchstone, 1997), p. 28.

11. Hansen, p. 193.

12. Frances Hill, *A Delusion of Satan: The Full Story of the Salem Witch Trials* (New York: Doubleday, 1995), pp. 178–179.

13. Hansen, p. 148.

14. Deborah Kent, *Salem Massachusetts* (Parsippany, N.J.: Dillon, 1996), p. 37.

15. Boyer and Nissenbaum, p. 8.

16. Hansen, pp. 150–151.

Chapter 8. "I Put an End to the Court"

1. Marion Starkey, *The Devil in Massachusetts: A Modern Enquiry into the Salem Witch Trials* (Garden City, N.Y.: Anchor, 1969), p. 213.

2. Carol F. Karlsen, *The Devil in the Shape of a Woman: Witchcraft in Colonial New England* (New York: Vintage, 1989), p. 41.

3. Chadwick Hansen, *Witchcraft at Salem* (New York: George Braziller, 1969), p. 163.

4. Enders Robinson, *The Devil Discovered: Salem Witchcraft 1692* (New York: Hippocrene, 1991), p. 232.

5. Paul Boyer and Stephen Nissenbaum, *Salem Possessed: The Social Origins of Witchcraft* (Cambridge, Mass.: Harvard University, 1974), p. 9.

6. Robinson, p. 236.

7. Kenneth Silverman, *The Life and Times of Cotton Mather* (New York: Harper and Row, 1984), p. 113.

8. Ibid., p. 118.

9. Hansen, p. 171.

10. Robinson, p. 227.

11. Hansen, p. 170.

12. Frances Hill, *A Delusion of Satan: The Full Story of the Salem Witch Trials* (New York: Doubleday, 1995), p. 117.

13. Ibid., p. 201.

14. Robinson, p. 244.

15. Ibid., p. 245.

Chapter 9. "Surviving Sufferers"

1. Richard B. Trask, *The Devil Hath Been Raised: A Documentary History of the Salem Village Outbreak of March 1692* (Danvers, Mass.: Yeoman, 1997), p. 125.

2. Marc Mappen, ed., *Witches and Historians: Interpretations of Salem* (Malibar, Fla.: Krieger, 1980), p. 30.

3. Ibid., p. 27.

4. Enders Robinson, *The Devil Discovered: Salem Witchcraft 1692* (New York: Hippocrene, 1991), p. 257.

5. Mappen, p. 70.

6. Kenneth Silverman, *The Life and Times of Cotton Mather* (New York: Harper and Row, 1984), p. 87.

7. Samuel F. Fowler, Esq., *An Account of the Life and Character of Rev. Samuel Parris of Salem Village and His Connections with the Witchcraft Delusion of 1692* (Salem, Mass.: The New England and Virginia Company, 1997), p. 11.

Chapter 10. "Swept Along by the Frenzy"

1. Richard B. Trask, *The Devil Hath Been Raised: A Documentary History of the Salem Village Witchcraft Outbreak of March 1692* (Danvers, Mass.: Yeoman, 1997), p. x.

2. Marc Mappen, ed., *Witches and Historians: Interpretations of Salem* (Malibar, Fla.: Krieger, 1980), pp. 36–37.

3. Deborah Kent, *Salem Massachusetts* (Parsippany, N.J.: Dillon, 1996), p. 28.

4. Trask, p. ix.

★ FURTHER READING ★

Books

Boyer, Paul, and Stephen Nissenbaum. *Salem Possessed: The Social Origins of Witchcraft*. Cambridge, Mass.: Harvard University, 1974.

Breslaw, Elaine G. *Tituba, Reluctant Witch of Salem: Devilish Indians and Puritan Fancies*. New York: New York University, 1996.

Editors of Time-Life Books. *Witches and Witchcraft*. Alexandria, Va.: Time-Life, 1990.

Hansen, Chadwick. *Witchcraft at Salem*. New York: George Braziller, 1969.

Hill, Frances. *A Delusion of Satan: The Full Story of the Salem Witch Trials*. New York: Doubleday, 1995.

Mofford, Juliet H. *Cry "Witch"—Salem 1692*. Carlisle, Mass.: Discovery Enterprises, 1995.

Roach, Marilynne K. *In the Days of the Salem Witchcraft Trials*. New York: Ticknor & Fields, 1996.

Robinson, Enders. *The Devil Discovered: Salem Witchcraft 1692*. New York: Hippocrene, 1991.

Starkey, Marion. *The Devil in Massachusetts: A Modern Enquiry into the Salem Witch Trials*. Garden City, N.Y.: Anchor, 1969.

Trask, Richard B. *The Devil Hath Been Raised: A Documentary History of the Salem Witchcraft Outbreak of March 1692*. Danvers, Mass.: Yeoman, 1997.

Zeinert, Karen. *The Salem Witchcraft Trials*. Danbury, Conn.: Franklin Watts, 1989.

Internet Addresses

National Geographic Society. *Salem Witchcraft Hysteria*. n.d. <http://www.nationalgeographic.com/features/97/salem/> (July 22, 1998).

Salem Witch Museum. July 17, 1998. <http://www.salemwitch museum.com/> (July 22, 1998).

★ INDEX ★